Beatlem

Beatlemania Lives On

Superfans in the 21st Century

DANA KLOSNER

McFarland & Company, Inc., Publishers

Jefferson, North Carolina

Unless otherwise noted, all photographs
were provided by the interviewee.

LIBRARY OF CONGRESS CATALOGUING-IN-PUBLICATION DATA

Names: Klosner, Dana, 1962– author.
Title: Beatlemania lives on : superfans in the 21st century / Dana Klosner.
Description: Jefferson, North Carolina : McFarland & Company, Inc.,
Publishers, 2023. | Includes index.
Identifiers: LCCN 2023024682 | ISBN 9781476690285 (paperback : acid free paper) ∞
ISBN 9781476650821 (ebook)
Subjects: LCSH: Beatles. | Rock music fans.
Classification: LCC ML421.B4 K62 2023 | DDC 782.42166092/2—
dc23/eng/20230605
LC record available at https://lccn.loc.gov/2023024682

BRITISH LIBRARY CATALOGUING DATA ARE AVAILABLE

ISBN (print) 978-1-4766-9028-5
ISBN (ebook) 978-1-4766-5082-1

On the cover: The Beatles (1964), Shown from left: Paul McCartney,
Ringo Starr, George Harrison, John Lennon (Photofest);
bottom left to right: Joy Cohen embracing Paul onstage after she got
his autograph (Joy Cohen); Ringo with Emily and her dad,
WFUV DJ Darren DeVivo, backstage at NYCB Theatre at Westbury
in NY (Darren DeVivo); Joe Kane dressed as barefoot Paul
on Abbey Road zebra crossing, surrounded by "George,"
"John," and "Ringo," and crowd down on one knee proposing
to Lindsay Humphreys Kane (Lindsay Kane)

Printed in the United States of America

*McFarland & Company, Inc., Publishers
Box 611, Jefferson, North Carolina 28640
www.mcfarlandpub.com*

For my beloved, beautiful late mom,
Lynn-e (don't forget the e!) Klosner,
who sadly passed just a few short months before publication.
My goal was to put this book in her hands.
She put up with my obsession my entire life.
Her famous words to me were
"You and those Beatles! You never give up!"
She was my biggest fan and cheerleader
since I was eight years old and wrote my first story,
"The Life of a Fly Inside a Ping Pong Ball."
This one's for you, Mom, with all my loving.

Table of Contents

Acknowledgments

This book is truly for the fans by a fan. The germ of the idea came to me when I visited Liverpool for the first time, rode the Magical Mystery Tour bus, and took in all the other incredible Beatles sights around the town. What fascinated me the most were the fans all around me. They came from all over the world, spoke many different languages, and were all different ages, with one thing in common—The Beatles. I knew that the fans would have amazing stories to tell, and they did not disappoint.

I want to thank everyone who participated in telling those stories. You each had a unique perspective, and as I had hoped, every one of you was so warm and friendly.

I need to thank my kids Bryan and Ollie Wehner for listening to all my crazy Beatles stories that I uncovered over the few years it took to write this book. It all started when Ollie off-handedly told me after all the writing I've done that I should write a book! So, I did.

I have to thank my dog Sammy for sitting by me during my phone interviews and making sure I got some quality outside time every day.

There are so many other people that it's hard to list just a few.

I want to thank Tony Award–winning Broadway producer Robin Gorman Newman. When I was kicking around the idea of the book, she told me that I really had something. She generously introduced me to many of her colleagues and friends who had The Beatles in their hearts and in their businesses. Without her encouragement this book might not exist.

I want to thank another Tony Award–winning Broadway producer, Vivek J. Tiwary, whom you will read about in these pages. He wrote the graphic novel *The Fifth Beatle* about Brian Epstein and began his research when he was a student at the Wharton School of Business, without any connections. Vivek told me that I reminded him of himself when he was researching Brian Epstein. I was touched and inspired by that remark.

I want to thank Joe Refano, of The Liverpool Shuffle, for introducing me to so many fans.

ix

Acknowledgments

I want to thank my sister and fellow writer, Jodi Levitan, for reading draft after draft, my cousin Rob Light for loving it and sharing with his colleagues, and one of my best friends, Bart Delio, for reading and encouraging me. Of course, to Margie Port-Hansen, Bonnie Hightower and Chris Burdick, I couldn't have done it without your love and support.

I need to thank a friend I call my Soda Man, Brian Siwulich, for keeping the faith and ultimately introducing me to Jeff Voesack, who led me on the right path to finding my publisher.

Special thanks to Susan Ryan for getting the whole ball rolling.

And perhaps most of all I want to thank the people at my wonderful publishing company, McFarland. Thank you to Dré Person for all his encouragement and thoughtful follow-up. Special thanks to company president Rhonda Herman for sharing my excitement about this project, accepting my manuscript and sharing it with the world.

I hope you all enjoyed the show!

Preface

*It All Started with a Trip
to the Promised Land—Liverpool*

When I started on this journey, I was a Beatles fan in a bubble. The only fans I knew were my kids, but they were not really fans by choice. People tolerated my obsession, but no one understood it. After being tormented in high school, I learned to hide my love away. As an adult, I kept my fandom on the back burner. But when I visited Liverpool for the first time and was surrounded by superfans just like me, I knew there was a story to tell. I set out to write a Beatles book like no other. It was not going to be historical or biographical; it was going to be about us—the superfans.

Living on suburban Long Island, I started my research, as everything in the 21st century begins, online. I simply typed in "Beatles walking tours in NYC" and lucked out: I met Beatles expert and Fab 4 NYC Walking Tours guide Susan Ryan. She was quick to reply and eager to be a part of my new endeavor. She lived in Queens, an hour away from me. I offered to interview her over the phone to avoid inconveniencing her and because I was nervous about meeting a "real expert" in person. I was thrilled and a little queasy when Susan suggested that we meet in person. She drove out to Long Island, and we met somewhere in the middle.

Warm and friendly, Susan immediately put me at ease. She was nothing like I expected of an expert; in fact, we had a lot in common. We were around the same age and became fans in the '70s. I had never before met anyone who shared my obsession, and I had an amazing time talking with her. Susan told me that being a fan in the '70s was tough for her. "It was totally uncool," she said. I could feel her pain. In high school I wore my fandom on my sleeve, literally, wearing Beatles T-shirts more often than not, which cemented my geek status. Everyone said they were old and broken up, move on; the Bee Gees and K.C. and the Sunshine Band—that was real music. Susan told me she loved all four Beatles, but she was most strongly connected to John. "People in school said mean things like 'He's old enough to be your father.'" But all these years later, she proudly looked me in the eye and said, "I feel vindicated." Back in the day, Susan shared Beatles music with anyone who would listen. I regaled her with stories of playing complete album sides over the phone for friends. My room was wallpapered with Beatles posters; looking at their beautiful faces soothed me. Susan nodded her head and hummed "mmm-hmm" in agreement.

After an hour I tried to wrap things up, afraid of taking up too much of her time. But Susan told me, as did everyone I interviewed, that The Beatles were her favorite subject. "I could talk about The Beatles all day long," she said, and I knew I'd met my Beatles sister.

When we were finished, Susan generously put me in touch with five other fans she was sure would want to be involved in my new book project. All five were as nice as she was and led me to more and more superfans by word of mouth. Since that first meeting with Susan, I've met Broadway and television producers working on Beatles projects and the director of Cavern City Tours, the umbrella company that runs the Magical Mystery Tour bus, International Beatleweek, and the Cavern Club in Liverpool. He treated me like royalty and gave me tickets to the Cavern Club and the Magical Mystery Tour bus. I have also interviewed the billionaire who cofounded the Liverpool Institute for Performing Arts with Paul McCartney. I found couples who met and married during International Beatleweek in Liverpool and tribute bands from all over the world.

The list of Beatles superfans is far too long to share here, but every one of them was as kind as Susan, giving me much more time than I'd ever hoped for and introducing me to more and more Beatles people. Beatles fans are the kindest and most generous people I have ever met. I am happy I have found my worldwide Beatles family. I've rediscovered my Beatles obsession through other people's eyes and now wear it proudly on my sleeve, T-shirt, or hat.

Now, if only I could get a hug from Paul. That's the next mission.

ONE

Catch Them with Another Fan

All you need are superfans.

The Oxford dictionary defines "superfan" as a person who has an extreme or obsessive admiration for a particular person or thing. What makes a superfan? Simply put, superfans know everything possible about the celebrities they worship and would do anything to get near them.

Before I started this book, I thought I was a superfan. Turns out I'm not even close to the superfans I met along the way. I am in awe and a bit jealous of the lengths superfans go to get a handshake, catch a glimpse, or even simply honor their favorite band, the best band in the world— THE BEATLES!

They Know His Name

"Get that f**king bike out of the way!" are the first words that David Stark, a music industry veteran in his 60s who hails from London, ever heard John Lennon say in person. David was a self-proclaimed nerdy 13-year-old, just after his bar mitzvah, and his bike was leaning on the gates of Abbey Road Studios. He and his bike didn't just show up there by chance. He knew that The Beatles were recording there that day, so he and his best friend and partner in crime—another boy named David— raced over there to catch a glimpse. Our David got a little more than he bargained for when John made the announcement through a speaker from his black Rolls-Royce limousine as he pulled up to the gates. David ran from the crowd of about 30 girls, moved his bike, and then watched as the limo parked and John got out of the car and ran up the steps.

"This was the era of 'Paperback Writer' and 'Rain,'" David told me on a transatlantic call from his home in London to mine in New York. "John was wearing cool sunglasses that were straight on top. It was a fantastic period, and he looked great."

As David regaled me with his story, I got lost in his English accent. To my untrained ear, he could have been a Beatle himself. But his is a London dialect, whereas theirs, of course, was Liverpudlian. To a native, the accents are probably as far apart as brash New Yorkese and a sweet southern drawl, but to me I could have been talking to Paul himself.

As a teenager in 1960s London, David had made a career out of gate-crashing, hovering outside courtroom doors, and staking out studios, homes, and offices until he started getting invitations to Beatles events. Almost 60 years later in the new millennium, Paul McCartney named him a companion of the Liverpool Institute for Performing Arts, the school Paul cofounded in 1996. Back in the States, that would be known as being given an honorary degree. Now David stands beside Paul at every graduation ceremony. Paul is there to shake hands with students, and David is there to bestow two lucky songwriting students with awards.

David's lifelong obsession started in 1963, when he was 10 years old, with the release of "Please Please Me." Like most of his entire generation, he was gobsmacked. The Beatles were new and different, and they topped the charts. David had to know everything about them and bought every fan magazine he could find. He started a scrapbook in

Left to right, David Stark, an unidentified woman who was walking by, George Harrison, and sax player Tom Scott. Outside Capitol Radio, 1974.

which he pasted pictures and articles. David worked in the music industry for 30 years as an international press officer for major record labels and later worked for Billboard/Music & Media and edited the magazine *Sound Engineer & Producer* before launching his own title in 1993, *SongLink International,* for songwriters and music publishers, which he still publishes online today. But nearly 60 years later, that childhood scrapbook is still David's prized possession.

As a child, David was immediately drawn to John. "He was a great singer, great performer, great character, and leader of the band," David said. But what really struck him about John was his dry wit. For instance, he said, "John loved the Goons [*The Goon Show*], a mad British television series that started on the radio in the 1950s. The Beatles would act like the Goons at times. I just loved how funny they were."

The Goon Show was a quick-witted, madcap show and the precursor to the likes of *Monty Python's Flying Circus* and other shows. John also loved Stanley Unwin, a British comedian who would change the words and spellings of everything, but his jibber-jabber always made hysterical sense in the end. That's what John did in his book *In His Own Write,* David noted. "He was a genius at doing that. He was so funny, and he was a great talker. He looked great and sounded great."

As a teen, David was brash enough to make sure he was in the right places at the right times to get up close and personal with The Beatles despite not being invited. David's own book about his adventures, *It's All Too Much,* was published in December 2020, but as one fan to another, he was kind enough to share some of his stories with me.

"My biggest adventure was when I gate-crashed the premiere of the *Yellow Submarine* film when I was 15 in 1968," he said. David and his friend, also named David but not the one of Abbey Road fame, both dressed in expensive suits to look the part for the occasion and "not like two nerds." They got to the theater in Piccadilly Circus hours before The Beatles were set to arrive and waited with the rest of the crowd. But our David was not one to follow the rules and gaze upon the band from afar. He was determined to get up close. His eyes darted around the theater looking for a way in, and when he spotted a man going in a door next to the main entrance, that was his shot.

The boys walked up to the door as if they belonged. To their amazement it wasn't locked, and it led to an unlocked elevator that took them to the top floor. From there it was a short flight of steps up to the roof. There was no security at all. There were quite a few people on the roof peering over the side watching the people below. At this point,

Piccadilly Circus was jammed with people and police. The VIPs started arriving by car. David had to get closer.

With chutzpah and a little luck, the Davids took the stairs down, which put them right into the top circle of the cinema while the stars were arriving. They were in! They walked all the way down to the dress circle where all of the celebrities were. The four Beatles walked in and took the front row. Photographers were going crazy. Paul and Jenny Boyd—sister of Pattie Boyd, George's first wife—entered together.

David scanned the VIP section and saw his opportunity when he spotted two empty seats in the second row, right behind The Beatles. Keith Richards, of the Rolling Stones, was sitting next to the two empty seats:

> There we are—15 years old—and we go up to him and ask, "Is anyone sitting here?"
>
> He says, "They're Mick and Marianne's seats [Mick Jagger, and his girlfriend at the time, Marianne Faithfull], but they're in New York, so you're okay." So I sit right behind Paul. John is to his right, then George and Ringo. It was incredible!
>
> After "Hey Bulldog," I said, "Oh, that's a good one."
>
> Paul heard me and said, "Oh, thank you."
>
> When the movie was over, it was mayhem. Everyone was trying to get near them, and they couldn't move. So we stood there chatting with John and George! I was 15! I can't remember anything we said.

That was just the beginning. Two days later David went to see his partner in crime, who lived in St. John's Wood near Abbey Road Studios.

"When I got out of the tube, I bumped into Paul!" Not the shy type, he went right up to Paul, started a conversation, and reminded him of things they had said a couple of nights before at the premiere. "He recognized me, and we had a chat. I had a clipping about the premiere in my back pocket, and he signed it for me."

Later in 1968, John and Yoko got busted for drug possession and had to go to court. David read the news and thought, *Oh boy*. The courthouse was nearby, and it was a Saturday so there was no school. David stood outside the courthouse with a crowd. Photographers were everywhere, and in the iconic photo of John and Yoko's arrival, David can be seen in the shot standing right behind them. That famous photo was all over the newspapers at the time, and now you can find it in many Beatles books. That drug bust led to complications years later when John tried to get his green card. In 1971, John left England and never went back. He thought that if he left the United States, he would not be able to get back in.

David tried his luck again when he saw a little item in the *New Musical Express* (a big music newspaper in 1960s England) about a contest for tickets to the Rolling Stones Rock & Roll Circus. There were thousands of entries and only 50 pairs of tickets. But it seemed as if everything David touched in those days turned to gold, and he won. On the bill were the Rolling Stones, The Who, Eric Clapton, and John Lennon. For some reason, David followed the rules that time and stayed in his seat, but he did see John perform "Yer Blues" from the *White Album*.

A few months later in 1969, David read about the premiere of the movie *The Magic Christian*, starring Peter Sellers and Ringo Starr. After his success at the *Yellow Submarine* premiere, David had no doubt he could get in, but he knew he needed a story. He dressed for success and headed to the cinema brimming with confidence. He walked along the red carpet straight to the box office and told the attendant that his aunt had left him a ticket. When the attendant asked his name, he had to think on the spot. "Benjamin Quincy Jones" came out of his mouth, though he had never even heard of Quincy Jones. The attendant told

Left to right, Paul McCartney and David Stark on LIPA graduation day, 2011.

him his name wasn't on the list. "I'm sure she would have left it," David insisted.

The attendant said she would have a word with the organizer. But wouldn't you know it? At that instant, the organizer was walking in with Princess Margaret, the Queen's sister. She walked toward and then past them into the cinema. "Oh, we'd better not bother her now," the attendant said. "Here's a ticket."

Once again, David had fudged his way in. And as if that weren't lucky enough, John and Yoko were outside the cinema protesting the innocence of an executed man. They were wearing black, and John talked to David animatedly about their cause.

John might have been his favorite, but David said George was the friendliest and most humble. In 1973, David went to the Capitol radio studio to catch George when he came out after an interview. The Beatle was happy to chat with the three or four people waiting there. Two months later, David's mother was given tickets to see Ravi Shankar. Onstage George introduced Ravi, and after the concert started David and his mother heard some shuffling behind them. "It was George!" said David. "He sat right behind us. He was nice and friendly, and he chatted with me and my mom. You could talk to him about anything. He was humble and modest, and he had a great sense of humor."

And so does David. The funniest story he told me was about the time he went to Ringo's house:

It was 1970. Ringo lived in Hampstead, a very smart area of London. I was at my friend's house. We weren't doing anything, and I said, "Why don't we go and find Ringo's house, see if he's in and ask him if he wants to go for a drink?" We knew what street he was on, but we didn't know the number. We rang the bell on the first house on the street. Ringo didn't answer, but Lulu, the singer who was married to Maurice Gibb of the Bee Gees at the time, did. Maurice followed behind her. We told them we were invited to Ringo's house, but we didn't know which one it was.

They said, "Oh, it's just down the road, the bottom one on the right." Can you even imagine that happening today?

We got to his house, and there were quite a few cars in the drive, so we knew he was home. We rang the bell. Ringo comes to the door holding a pool cue. We were dressed in hippie clothes, afghan coats, and the whole thing. He said, "Hello, lads. What can I do for you?"

I said, "Do you fancy coming to the pub for a drink?"

He said, "Sorry, I've got friends in tonight." And as he was saying it, I saw Eric Clapton walk by behind him!

8

One. Catch Them with Another Fan

As a tween, David was one of the chosen ones who got to see The Beatles perform together. Better yet, it was not in a huge stadium but at the Hammersmith Odeon, the largest cinema in London, capacity 3,500. His dad knew an accountant in the music business, and that was their in. It was one of the Christmas shows in 1965. David and his family were in the front balcony, but even in this small space they couldn't hear anything above the screaming. The Beatles were not the only ones on the bill. The Yardbirds, Eric Clapton, and lots of other well-known '60s bands played. "The Beatles did this funny sketch where they wore furry outfits, and they were searching for the Abominable Snowman. They really could have been clowns," David said.

David has been immersed in The Beatles' world for as long as he can remember. He's even spent time with John's aunt Mimi, who raised John. David met her through an invitation from an American pen pal, Cathy, whom he met through the pen pal section of The Beatles' monthly book back in the 1960s. Cathy had been corresponding with Mimi for a few years and met her in Liverpool on a trip she took around 1965. They got on famously and continued writing to each other for years. When Cathy went back to England to see Mimi in 1981 shortly after John was killed, she asked David to join her. "I brought flowers, and we got on very well," David said. "Even though she wasn't his mother, she had the same look and the same sense of humor."

David's whole career has been inspired by his love for the band. He translated his love for music into a career in publicity at music magazines and record labels. Because of his positions, he was able professionally to get up close and personal with the guys during their solo careers as well as with many other iconic musicians. On one occasion, David reminded Paul McCartney of their meeting at the *Yellow Submarine* premiere. Paul only vaguely remembered.

David's love for The Beatles also steered him toward being a musician. Seeing John Lennon that fateful day outside Abbey Road Studios inspired him to learn to play the drums, and he has been playing ever since. David's music career has led him to be part of many Beatles and solo Beatles tribute bands. Today he is in the Trembling Wilburys, a Traveling Wilburys tribute. Like the Beatles themselves, David is also a talented songwriter. He parlayed his skill into running a website called SongLink International, where songwriters can meet music producers. "It's like a dating app for songwriters," he joked.

"My life is wrapped up with The Beatles, and I love it," he lovingly said. "I can't get away from them."

To read more of David's adventures, look for his book *It's All Too Much* at www.ItsAllTooMuch.net.

When She Saw Him Standing There

Julie Hemmert was a guest at the White House
when Paul performed for 200 people, including the Obamas.

When she was just 17—you know what I mean—in the 1970s, Julie wore a locket around her neck with a picture of Paul McCartney inside it. On June 2, 2010, he kissed her cheek at the White House when President Barack Obama was in office. It was the happiest day of her life but so surreal that sometimes she still can't believe it happened.

How did Julie Hemmert of Cincinnati get to be a guest at the White House, where Paul was awarded the Library of Congress Gershwin Prize

Paul on stage at the White House during the "Hey Jude" performance on June 2, 2010. Some well-known people on stage, left to right, are David Grohl, Obama's daughter Sasha, President Obama, Paul himself, Jerry Seinfeld, and Stevie Wonder (courtesy Kelly Schaefer).

for Popular Song? She was among just 200 people, including the Obamas; Paul's wife, Nancy; his brother, Mike; and his children.

The long and winding road goes back to Chicago, where Barack Obama lived before his presidency. His then— deputy associate director of the Office of the Social Secretary, Cookie Offerman, is a Chicago native, which is how she knew of Beatle expert and host of *Breakfast with the Beatles* Terri Hemmert, of Chicago's popular radio station WXRT. It's no coincidence that Terri and Julie share a last name; Terri happens to be Julie's older sister.

Paul at the piano in the East Room of the White House performing "Let It Be" on June 2, 2010 (courtesy Kelly Schaefer).

On February 9, 1964, Julie, then four years old, sat on Terri's lap watching *The Ed Sullivan Show*. Julie says she doesn't remember details of the show, but Terri, at 15, was hooked and took Julie along on the Beatlemania ride. Cookie knew Terri should be at the White House the night Paul received his award, and Terri knew Julie had to be there.

"I freaked out totally when she invited me," Julie, 62, said. "I spent $800 on a flight. I would've walked there, it meant so much to me."

Julie arrived in Washington, D.C., the morning of the performance. Terri was set to arrive two hours later. But as Murphy's Law would have it, Terri's flight was canceled due to bad weather. Julie panicked. "What if I was turned away at the gate? What if Paul got sick and couldn't perform? What if Terri didn't make it in time? What if Paul turned out to be an a-hole?"

Terri finally arrived at 4:00, two hours before they were set to be at the White House. Julie calmed down, just a little.

From there it was all a dream. Julie and Terri arrived at the east entrance to the White House at 6:00. The line was small—only about 25 people—but security was tight. Each guest went through three points where identifications were checked against the guest list. After the scrutiny, they were sent through a metal detector.

When Julie passed through the metal detector, the dream became a reality. *"I was in!!"* she exclaimed. This was really going to happen.

Guests were treated like VIPs from the moment they arrived. They enjoyed champagne as they mingled. Then it was time. Julie was tingling with excitement as they were escorted into the East Room. "You see the East Room on TV all the time," Julie said. "There was a portrait of George and Martha Washington on the wall and a small makeshift stage just a couple of feet off the ground. In front of that, there were only four rows!" Julie and Terri took seats in the second row. "There were all these important people there … and me! It was very intimate. The

Julie Hemmert's teenage bedroom, circa 1977.

Obamas came in and got seated. Then Paul comes in and sits next to Barack Obama. I was literally just a few feet from him! It was wild to see him that close!"

Julie was devastated that she didn't have a camera to capture the moment. She was told cameras weren't allowed. But all was not lost. Apparently, another guest didn't get the memo. She had a camera and took great pictures. In addition, the concert was captured for the world by PBS,

Julie Hemmert's photograph of Paul onstage performing June 2, 2010, in the East Room at the White House. President and Michelle Obama are seen in the audience (courtesy Kelly Schaefer).

which was on hand to record the event. You can catch glimpses of Julie in the film. "I was the dreamy-eyed 13-year-old watching the whole thing."

Julie's heart went boom when Paul crossed that room, walking that "Beatle walk" just a few feet in front of her, and took the stage. "We were so close to Paul that when he played 'Let It Be,' I could see his fingers on the piano!"

Julie was just as close to Paul when he was offstage, and she dreamily gazed at him while he watched iconic recording artists perform his songs. "He was mouthing the words!" She said incredulously.

Paul ended the show with the now-famous "Hey Jude" performance. All of the artists and the Obamas got onstage and sang along. Politicians and other invited guests joined in as well.

Then it was over.

Or was it?

"The First Family left," Julie said, "but Paul was hanging out. My sister has interviewed him a few times, but she never assumes he knows who she is. She went right up to him and said, 'I'm Terri Hemmert, WXRT. I've interviewed you a few times. This is my sister. She sat on my lap when we watched *Ed Sullivan*.' I was trying to keep calm. I was freaking out inside. I said, 'Congratulations on your award, and I really enjoyed your concert tonight.'"

That's when the unimaginable happened.

"He took both my hands in his and kissed me on my left cheek!" Julie said. Terri told her that she'd never seen Paul do that when he meets a fan. "He was excited about the award. It meant a lot to him; I could tell," Julie said. "He was so kind. He waited after the concert to talk with some of the people that lingered. I even got a picture of me with Paul, my sister, and Larry Kane." Larry Kane is an American journalist who famously toured with The Beatles in 1964 and has written numerous books about them.

"It isn't often that you meet your idol, and he is so kind," said Julie. "I get teary-eyed thinking about it. He could've just left the room. Of all the fans I've ever met, I've never heard a bad Paul story. He is always very kind to everybody. All these years and he is still kind. I love him even more for that."

Julie could hardly sleep when she got back to the hotel. The emotions poured out when she got back home to Cincinnati, put her key in her car's ignition and The Beatles were playing on a CD she had left in the player. "I bawled my eyes out," she said. She was done holding it all in. "It was the best night of my life . . . better than I would have ever thought."

When Julie thought it over, she said lovingly, "He gets it. My sister told me he gets it. People are born, get married, and die to his music. It comforts them. He gets that."

The Beatles' music bonded the three Hemmert sisters when they were kids. Tragically, their youngest sister, Joni, was killed in a car accident when she was 19. The lyrics from "In My Life" were imprinted on her prayer card, and Beatles music was played at her funeral.

It's because of that kind of love for the music that Julie is still known as "the Beatles fanatic" to all her friends from high school and college. When James Corden's "Carpool Karaoke" segment with Paul was set to air, she got tons of instant messages, texts, and phone calls to alert her to the event. As if she didn't already know.

To this day and forward, Beatles music and Paul McCartney have filled and will continue to fill Julie's life, her relationships, and her soul.

Who Knows How Much She Loves Him

Maria Tuttle's goal is to get that Paul hug,
and she's come darn close.

"I love you, Paul!" Maria Tuttle shouted across a crowded room. "I love you too!!" Paul shouted back. The world stopped. She would never be the same. And her husband was just as excited as she was. Well, almost.

Maria and Bob were in fifth-row seats at a concert in Hershey, Pennsylvania. Maria, a fan since she was two months shy of five years old, has had lots of other brushes with her favorite Beatle. "He made

Maria Tuttle's photograph of Paul waving from his limo during a Limo Watch. September 2017 at Nassau Coliseum in Uniondale, New York.

eye contact with me once!" she said, still amazed that it happened. "In 1984, he was at a premiere on First Avenue in New York City. I stood there with my sister for five or six hours. He got out of a car with Linda. He looked right at me. We made eye contact for a second. It was really exciting!"

Maria's ultimate dream is to meet the man himself and tell him what he has meant to her all her life. Well, really, her ultimate dream since she was two months shy of age five has been to marry Paul. When I asked how her love for him has grown and matured over the last 50-odd years, she simply said it hasn't. "I still want to marry Paul. Nothing's changed."

Maria continually tries to be in the same place at the same time as Paul—some might call it good-natured stalking—to proclaim her love or at least to say hello. Living on Long Island means it wasn't a far trek to Montauk Point—the end of the island—to vacation there for a week close to Paul's home in Amagansett. Maria and her husband, Bob, spent the week riding bikes near Paul's house and hanging out at his favorite coffeehouse. No luck. They did see Paul's daughter Stella three times but no Paul. As luck would have it, it turns out Paul was there just a couple of weeks later.

While tooling around the neighborhood, the couple spotted a tag sale just around the corner from Paul's house. The woman there said she had met her neighbor Paul, and he was really sweet and nice. She had told Paul "I saw you at Shea Stadium."

And Paul joked back, "Oh, that was you in the front row. I remember."

Most recently, Maria and Bob stood in Grand Central Station for three hours after Paul teased fans on *The Tonight Show Starring Jimmy Fallon* that he would be playing a surprise concert at a station in New York, and it would be "grand." He was there promoting his new album at the time, *Egypt Station*, which debuted at number one on the *Billboard* charts in 2018.

"There was a rumor that you could get in [to the show] with a number on a MetroCard. My husband bought a card the day before. Paul's dressing room was in the Met Life building. He could either walk across the station or drive to 42nd Street and go in that way. We guessed he was going to walk across the station. We thought driving in the city would be too much of a hassle, so we stayed put." The excitement built when security parted the crowd and made an aisle. "We were right in the front! Nancy came in. We were sure he would follow behind," Maria said.

Unfortunately, he didn't. Paul was driven around the corner and entered through a different door. But Maria still wasn't sure as she stood waiting for her idol. "We heard the music start. We didn't know if it was live or a movie or what." But when she saw the livestream on YouTube, she knew that night wasn't meant to be.

The Grand Central show was free, but Maria has paid big bucks for the chance to come that much closer to speaking to the man himself, hoping to maybe even win a hug. In 2016, she and Bob plunked down thousands of dollars for the chance to watch a sound check before the concert in Hershey, Pennsylvania. Prior to that day, a friend of hers had been called onstage. "On Facebook, she's singing with him!" With hope beyond hope, Maria thought this would happen to her. She carried a sign that read "Please Please Me, I Need a Hug." Sadly, she wasn't among the lucky few to be called onstage, but she was there for the sound check. Her only disappointment was that she wasn't able to stand as close to him as she'd hoped. Paul kept everyone back by the soundboard, saying the sound quality was better there.

"He played lots of Beatles songs, Carl Perkins, and others," Maria said. "He played for about 45 minutes, before a three-hour show!"

Maria is a self-proclaimed Paul fanatic but reports that some of the people there were crazier than she is. "People came from all over the world to go to each concert," she said. "They follow him around and go to every sound check. There was even a girl that had nine or 10 Beatles tattoos."

Of course, Maria

Maria Tuttle daydreaming of seeing The Beatles live at the Cavern Club while standing in front of the club in Liverpool, November 2016.

17

and Bob have made the pilgrimage to Liverpool. Must-see attractions for any Beatles fan in Liverpool are Paul and John's childhood homes that have been donated to the National Trust and are open for tours. The homes are modest to say the least. As everyone knows, The Beatles did not grow up entitled. Paul grew up in a row house at 20 Forthlin Road, reminiscent of the row houses in Baltimore, Maryland. John grew up in a posher part of town. His childhood home has a name: Mendips. Still, it's a small semidetached house. Both homes are now museums and have been restored to depict the way the lads grew up. The rooms in both these houses are small and cramped, although Mendips is slightly larger than 20 Forthlin Road. In both kitchens, you have just enough room to turn around. John's and Paul's bedrooms were both the size of closets, barely fitting their twin beds, dressers, and guitars.

As a sidenote, the first time I visited Liverpool in 2004, the tours of John's and Paul's childhood homes were quite informal. You were given headphones for an audio tour. In Paul's house his voice guided you from room to room, filling you in on all the details as if you were his old friend. A caretaker lived in each of the homes and quietly stood back,

Maria Tuttle's photograph of Paul onstage from her very close vantage point, September 2017, Nassau Coliseum.

letting fans enjoy taking it all in. When I got to Paul's bedroom, the caretaker was there. He looked at me and said, "Go on." I didn't understand. Then he said, "'You know you want to." He looked from me to Paul's bed. Again he said, "Go on." *Is he saying what I think he saying?* I wondered. Then I touched it! I was touching Paul's bed! "Give it a go!" he said. I laid down! There I was lying on Paul McCartney's bed! How could this be real?! I don't have a picture, but that memory is etched indelibly in my memory.

John lived in Mendips with his aunt Mimi, who never took his dream to be a musician seriously. "Playing the guitar is all very well, John, but you'll never make a living at it," she's famously quoted as saying. When Paul came around to play guitar with John, she sent them out to the entrance room and closed the door. Paul's father, Jim, was just the opposite. He was a musician and enthusiastically encouraged their dream. Needless to say, they practiced at Paul's house more often. John and Paul wrote "She Loves You" in the parlor at Paul's house, then stepped into the living room and played it for Jim. He said it was a fine song, but "Yeah, yeah, yeah" was too American. They should say "Yes, yes, yes."

I felt Maria's excitement as she told me about her own experience in their homes. She was astonished by the size of Paul's childhood home, especially his bedroom. "To think that he still lived there after achieving Beatles fame!" she exclaimed. Despite its size, knowing that she was in the home where Paul grew up was thrilling. "You know you read about it, but then you see it, and it's preserved in time!"

Maria and Bob met their tribe of Beatles fanatics by following a Long Island tribute band called the Liverpool Shuffle. It's a group that she feels captures The Beatles. The band enjoys their own superfans, who are all fast friends. "The whole group socializes," Maria said. "Some of us go to lunch. We text each other and keep in touch. We say if we're going to go see the Liverpool Shuffle."

When Maria told me about the sound check, I'd never heard of it. Apparently, before most concerts Paul plays for an audience of about 100 people. I *had* to go! I got a job so I wouldn't have to take money out of savings to pay for tickets. I was prepared to travel anywhere in the country. But as soon as the tickets went on sale, they were sold out. I was extremely lucky, though. I have a dear cousin in the music business who got me into the sound check and the concert at Dodger Stadium in Los Angeles during the 2019 Freshen Up tour. Ringo Starr was a special guest at the concert. Ringo and Paul played "Helter

Skelter" and the "Sgt. Pepper's Lonely Hearts Club Band" reprise. Tears rolled down my cheeks. It is because of Maria (and the generosity of my cousin) that I was there. I want to thank Maria for showing me the way.

For me, Maria and millions of fans around the world, The Beatles are a way of life.

She Said When It's His Birthday

The baby was due June 30, 2017. At 38 weeks, on June 17, Beth Wardell's water broke at a prenatal checkup. She would have to have her labor induced to avoid infection, the doctor told her.

"Not today," Beth said. She waited till the following day. Why? Because she wanted her baby to be born on Paul McCartney's birthday: June 18.

Some may say Beth's a dreamer. When she learned that her due date was June 30, she prayed her baby would be born on a Beatle's birthday. With Paul's birthday on June 18 and Ringo's on July 7, June 30 was right in the middle. Through a little finagling, she got her wish. It's no accident that she named her little boy Jude and plays The Beatles' "Good Night" as a lullaby at bedtime. A year later, Beth had a little girl. Her water broke on John Lennon's birthday, but this baby didn't come until two days later. Her name: Eleanor.

Long before she became a young wife and mother, Beth was a fan. She was born a Mormon in Salt Lake City, Utah, in

Beth Wardell's son Jude, born on Paul's birthday, as a newborn wearing a shirt that reads "Hey Me, I'm Jude," in 2017.

1990. Beatles music opened her eyes and took her outside of her "Utah bubble." The Beatles' voices helped shape her inner thoughts. "I can say with fair certainty their voices are the ones I am most familiar with," she said. "Their voices are literally a part of me."

In a world where most people choose family names, naming her children after Beatles songs seemed right. The Beatles "don't know who I am, but they are my family," Beth said. "It made more sense than going five generations back. The Beatles are more of a connection, and they mean more to me. It felt like a family name." It makes Beth happy when friends say "Hey Jude" to her little one. When he was just a few months old, she dressed him in a onesie that said "Hey Me—I'm Jude."

Beth's Beatles obsession is not a generational thing. There were no older fans in her family. She became a fan with a little help from her friend Rachel. Before Rachel showed her the way, Beth thought The Beatles were "old hippie music." Rachel was relentless and constantly played the music. She knew she'd break down Beth's resistance completely if Beth saw The Beatles moving around and heard them joking in a movie. She was right; one viewing of *Help!* and Beth was gone.

Now Beth says there's nothing better than Paul in concert. "When Paul plays 'Let It Be,' it's a near-religious experience," she said. "Those [concerts] are some of the best memories of my life. I can't believe that man is in his 70s [now in his 80s]!"

It's not just what's onstage that feels like home to Beth; it's the fans. Stadiums are filled with fans of all ages, she said. "The original Beatles fans dance to 'Ob-La-Di, Ob-La-Da' and sit during the rest. What is incredible is that people my age shell out that kind of money to see a 70-year-old man play decades-old songs. Little kids are there and are into it too." Utah fans come from as far away as Idaho and Wyoming, and Beth says there's "tremendous energy" at the concerts.

With two of the members gone, Beth is anxious about Paul and Ringo's mortality. She hopes that when they die, their heads and brains are put on robotic bodies and they keep going forever. I think she was only half joking.

It Was a Hard Day's Night

"I saw him walking through the store," said Rachel Bremilst of Massachusetts regarding a record signing she went to in London.

Rachel and her then-husband waited outside HMV Records in Oxford Square London all night to secure their spot. It was like a scene out of *A Hard Day's Night*. Fans of all ages filled the sidewalks on both sides of the street and spilled onto the median, hoping for a chance to get Sir Paul's autograph. After sleeping all night on a makeshift bed of cardboard she found in an alley and a blanket they snagged from the hotel where they'd spent the night before, Rachel found herself 11th in line. This was really going to happen.

When Rachel made her way inside the store it looked like all record stores at the time, with aisle after aisle of records and CDs except there was Paul's head bobbing through the aisles. She started hyperventilating, unable to believe that she was breathing the same air as her love. Though her heart went boom, she was able to memorize what Paul McCartney looked like walking. He had short hair and was wearing a blazer over his shirt. He looked youthful, friendly, funny, and happy just as he'd looked onstage, online, and in the movies during all of the years since 1979 when she'd fallen in love with him at age 10. Paul was comfortable stepping up to the two-step stage, and he seemed to be genuinely pleased to be chatting with everyone.

"There was a platform they were using for a stage. He got up and sat behind the table. I was hyperventilating. I was trying to hold it together. I was wearing a tie-dye shirt that said 'And in the end, the love you take is equal to the love you make' [a famous lyric from 'The End' part of the *Abbey Road* medley]. Then it was my turn," Rachel said. "They took

Bride and groom Rachel Bremilst and her former husband cutting their Beatles wedding cake, September 8, 1996.

my camera and all my bags. All I had were the things for him to sign. I climbed a couple of steps up to his table."

Meeting her idol, Sir Paul McCartney, was truly a surreal moment for Rachel. As she was growing up, her parents owned a florist shop and were busy. On weekends, Rachel was left to entertain herself. She had never heard of The Beatles. Her mom loved Johnny Cash, and her dad was into polka music. She found *Yellow Submarine* just by chance, flipping channels while lying on the new shag rug in her small living room. A quiet but happy child, Rachel loved the cartoon and bopped along to the music, having no idea that The Beatles were behind the animation. She didn't stand a chance when the boys made their real-life appearance at the end.

"Oh my God, they're real!" It was like a lightning bolt; her little mind was blown. Rachel begged her mom to take her to a record store so she could buy her very first record, the *Yellow Submarine* album. After playing it constantly, she found out there was more where that came from. Sure, she liked other bands like Sha Na Na and David Bowie, but The Beatles were something special. She bought as many books, posters, and albums as she could find. She covered her walls with pictures that she cut out of a book so she could look at them all the time. She found herself gazing at Paul the most.

"He was adorable, had a beautiful voice, he was a vegetarian and he included Linda in his life," Rachel said in our telephone interview while her teenage son, Paul—yes, named after him—in the next room was playing video games. "He and I just clicked."

Paul—McCartney that is—inspired Rachel to become a vegetarian for 20 years, and she attributes that to her healthier life. What appealed to Rachel when she was 10 were the melodies, the upbeat, happy, peppy songs that were easy to sing along to. As a teen, her thoughts turned to romance. She fondly remembered that when she began dating her first boyfriend, they named "Here, There and Everywhere" their song.

When Rachel stood in front of Paul in that record shop in London in 1977, he said to her, "Oh, I like your shirt."

She barely heard him as she struggled to keep it together. *Shirt? I'm wearing a shirt?* went through her head. What finally came out of her mouth was "My shirt, oh yeah."

Rachel handed Paul her record to sign, and he said, "Who should I make it out to?"

She muttered, "Oh ... um ... Rachel."

In a crystallizing moment, Rachel realized this was the chance of a lifetime. She had to say something intelligent. With all her gumption, she told her lifelong idol and heartthrob, "You inspired me to be a vegetarian.... We just had a Beatles wedding last year."

Paul said in return, "Oh, did ya? Thanks for coming out today. I really appreciate it."

"Then, in slow motion, he puts his hand out," Rachel said. She continued: "His hand was going toward me so I could shake it. And I'm looking at him. I'm gonna get to touch him! The moment went on forever. I shook his hand! It was really strong, and soft, and warm, and it smelled great! I'd given him the letter (that I wrote back in America in case I lost it). He said, "Oh, I'll make sure to read this letter." Then my moment was over, and they escorted me aside. That's when I absolutely lost it. I was crying and shaking. All the emotions I was holding in came out. I didn't want to lose it in front of him. That would be bad. I didn't want to be one of those fans."

That might have been the end of Rachel's moment but not her story. When it was her husband's turn and Paul asked him "Who should I make it out to?" he said, "Can you make it out to my wife? That's her over there losing her shit. She really loves you."

And Paul said, "You're a good man."

So now Rachel has two autographed albums to commemorate the moment and to prove to herself that it wasn't a dream. And that Beatles wedding she told Paul about? Well, it was so extravagant that it was written up in the *Boston Herald*.

Plans for that wedding started taking shape the moment she said yes. As thoughts of decorations and flowers filled her head, Rachel remembered The Beatles wedding she had been dreaming of since she was 10. Her fiancé was happy to go along for the ride.

Rachel got busy shopping for Beatles merchandise from her Fest for Beatles Fans catalog, an annual festival in New York, but she didn't have to order everything by mail. In the mid–1990s, a new flood of Beatles memorabilia hit the stores. She ordered Beatles buttons from the catalog and bought Beatles bubblegum cards from the local grocery store. The store manager gave her the life-size cardboard cutout of the boys that they used for a display when the sale was over. She was a very crafty bride after years of working in her parents' florist shop. She decoupaged the seating cards with the bubblegum cards, each of which had a picture of one of the boys. The buttons went into the men's boutonnieres and bridesmaids' bouquets. The life-size display was the first thing the guests saw when they walked into the banquet hall foyer. The cake was elaborate, with two separate staircases. On every step were groomsmen and bridesmaids figurines. The top of the staircases were the top layer with the bride and groom cake topper, and at the foot of the two staircases was a platform where figurines of The Beatles jammed onstage.

Guests knew what they were in for when they got the invitation, which, just like Rachel's shirt on that fateful day, read "And in the end, the love you take is equal to the love you make."

Some of Rachel's family and friends rolled their eyes, and people on the groom's side of the family probably wondered what he was getting himself into, Rachel said. But a lot of their guests were Beatles friends and told her it was the most fun they'd ever had at a wedding.

The bride's Beatlemania dream did not end when the final notes were played at the reception. By some weird coincidence, their honeymoon in Nova Scotia coincided with a tour by Pete Best's band. Pete was The Beatles' first drummer before Ringo replaced him in 1962. The couple told their waiter they were newlyweds, and as a honeymoon surprise, they got to meet Pete Best and the rest of the band.

That still wasn't enough for this die-hard megafan. Since then, Rachel has followed Paul around the world and seen him in concert 75 times since 1989. Yes, I said 75! But she's not made of money. When traveling to a show, she lives on peanut butter sandwiches and sleeps in airports. "I'll go as far as my money will take me," said Rachel, whose favorite show is always the last one she has seen. Rachel met Ringo at another record signing, and she even met the late George Martin, The Beatles' record producer.

As for Rachel's son, Paul, he is far from embarrassed by his mom's superfandom. He's actually proud to be McCartney's namesake. The Beatles were the first band he ever listened to, and he appreciates them to this day. He wore Beatles T-shirts in high school, and in the new millennium they are cool again. "Paul's a generic name," Paul Bremilst said, "but when I tell the story, it always gets a hoot." Some of his music teachers in high school and college asked if he was named for McCartney before he even had the chance to tell them.

For a lifetime The Beatles have given Rachel joy and comfort, and they've led her to the best friends and experiences of her life.

"I wouldn't be who I am today if it weren't for them," she said. "And their message is more important now than ever. Give peace a chance, for God's sake."

Her Father Should Know

Second-generation fan.

"We stalked [Paul's] hotel, and he gave us a wave!" said starstruck Liz Czapaski Hiron. Just two days after her wedding, she left her new husband behind and went to see Paul McCartney with her best friend.

In her 40s, Liz is a second-generation fan. She fell in love with the band in 2000, when she was 12. She was born in the late '70s, so you might think she's too young to love The Beatles. She missed it all. But she and fans of her generation prove that the Fab Four are timeless in their appeal. The music gets by with a little help from its friends. The torch is passed from father to daughter, from grandmother to grandchild, from fan to emerging fan. Liz's love for The Beatles might have even started in the womb. Her father grew up in the '60s. "He loved The Beatles. I thought they were creepy crawly things," she said.

The Beatles album *1*, a compilation album released in late 2000, introduced a new generation to the band, but Liz already knew and liked the songs thanks to her father. *The Beatles Anthology* got her hooked, and she had to know more. Who were the guys behind the music? What were their personalities? The more she learned about them, the more smitten she was with George. "He was funny. He was very witty when

Liz Czapaki Hiron, who got a wave out of a hotel room from Paul McCartney, hugging the statue of John Lennon on Matthew Street in Liverpool, 2009.

Liz Czapaki Hiron happily stands by her favorite—George—in front of the busts of our boys on the wall at the Cavern Club in Liverpool, 2009.

interviewed, and he had a great presence onstage. He was fun to watch! He was the most beautiful man I ever saw."

And the more Liz got into George, the more she got into each Beatle. "The band has been broken up for 50 years, and I'm still learning new things," she said in awe.

In the year 2000 kids weren't into The Beatles, and Liz felt like an outsider with her classmates, but she persisted in her fandom. It was important to her to establish something in a unique time. At the turn of the new millennium, other kids were into the Backstreet Boys and the Spice Girls. Liz says she tried to force herself to get into Harry Potter. "You can't force what you don't like."

Liz sought friends in other places. She met Beatles friends from around the world online on a now-defunct forum called Beatle Links. She met all sorts of people, many older and even some younger than she was. It was there that she met Beatles expert Susan Ryan, who ran a fan fiction page. For a while "I would read the page, but I didn't submit," Liz said. Then she got into the act, writing romantic comedies about the boys. "They were such comedians at heart. I wrote funny things that happened on tour and romantic things."

As she got older, Liz realized what an impact The Beatles had had on an entire generation. "They were politically and culturally important," she said. "They were singing and preaching about love. Not too many other music groups have such a positive influence."

Love for The Beatles has deepened the love between Liz and her father too. "My dad taught me so much," she said. "He has Beatles toys and wigs, and he remembers watching them on *Ed Sullivan*." And now Liz is passing the torch. "I'm subtly introducing them to my daughter. There are Beatles records and Beatles books on the shelf. I will point to them and say 'Beatles,' but I won't pressure her."

"For the last 15 years, The Beatles have always been in my life," Liz said. "Through all my ups and downs, their songs and messages have motivated me. They've always been present. A couple of months might go by where I don't listen to their music or read a Beatles book, but then a song will come on, and it will feel like the first time. Just like their song, 'I'm in love for the first time, don't you know it's gonna last!' They are forever classic and forever eternal."

The Band's Story Launched Her Career

Budding journalist and Beatles fanatic Grace Hebron, age 24, landed her first freelance assignment with a Beatles story. Okay, a story inspired by The Beatles, but still it was a written in the stars that her journalism career in Baltimore was off to a great start.

At the height of the COVID-19 pandemic, Baltimore's nonprofit adult album–oriented radio station WTMD wanted to bring live music back to the city. Station executives, too young to actually remember The Beatles' rooftop concert, jumped to the idea of a Beatles-inspired concert theme. They wanted to do something outdoors, in public, where listeners could socially distance. Logistically a rooftop wouldn't work, but keeping with the theme, they decided to hold a concert on a ship that floated throughout the Inner Harbor of Baltimore. When Grace was hired to write about the event for *Baltimore Magazine*, she knew exactly what the show's producers were going for. She opened with setting the scene of the "wind-whipped" day The Beatles played their final concert on the rooftop of Apple Corps headquarters on January 30, 1969. Even though she was born in 1997, she knew every nuance of what happened on the rooftop—at least the nuances that appeared on the videos she fervently watched on YouTube while growing up.

"I still think that's one of the best stories I've ever written," she said. "It was so inspired. And the whole idea of them doing that and bringing live music back is such a love letter to The Beatles."

Much like The Beatles' rooftop concert, WTMD's floating concert was difficult to bring to fruition, but it was monumental. It was just as monumental for Grace. A recent college graduate, she just started on her journalistic journey, and her first story was a tribute to the band she's been obsessed with,

Grace Hebron wears a huge smile as she holds Paul's *McCartney II* album cover in her hand, 2022.

researching, and listening to since middle school. For Grace, things are getting better all the time. She has since been hired full-time as assistant editor at *Baltimore Magazine.*

Let's back up a little bit. Cut to preteen Grace happily bopping along to Beatles music that her dad played in the car.

"I always knew who they were and that they were huge. I just never knew that I loved them," Grace said.

Grace can't pinpoint the moment she fell in love, but like most of us, she was around 12 years old. But according to her dad, her obsession started much earlier than that.

"My dad said even when I was a baby 'Wonderful Christmastime' was my favorite. And it's still not Christmas unless I listen to that song."

From "Ob La Di, Ob La Da," to *Abbey Road*, The Beatles were the soundtrack Grace grew up with when she went on family vacations or was shuttled around to the activities that molded her childhood.

"My dad would play *Abbey Road* in the car, and it was always fascinating," Grace said. "'Across the Universe' is a song that if you hear it when you're 12, you're going to think 'What is this?' It's kind of an earful. I can't pinpoint the jumping point of when it was like 'I'm going to listen to every single Beatles album there is. Because that's what I did. I went from beginning to end. I went from *A Hard Day's Night* era to *Rubber Soul*."

In her middle and high school years Grace spent many a late night into the wee morning hours researching, learning everything she could about the boys, their music, their philosophies, their lives, their wives, their children, and their grandchildren. At 24, she can stand toe-to-toe with any first-generation fan; she is almost encyclopedic in her knowledge. But what is fascinating is that while most first- and second-generation fans learned from listening, reading books and magazines, and watching TV, movies, and DVDs, her knowledge comes in a more 21st-century way.

"When I was a teen, a lot of [information] was on [the social media platform] Tumblr. I would spend hours on Tumblr looking at Beatles-related stuff. You could find rare pictures, quotes, and stories. It's kind of crazy how many people my age were also obsessed. People in my generation are huge on fandoms. That's a culture that the internet facilitates where people can connect on any subject on any platform. Search Paul McCartney on Instagram and there's bound to be 40 or 50 pages that are run by girls in their teens or 20s who compile old pictures and captions daily. They post their thoughts about him or the music. You'll find photos that you wouldn't get if you Googled him. I don't know where they get them. They might be old film stills or video stills. These fangirls go deep."

Grace also watched all the YouTube videos she could find. She recorded the Wings documentary "One Hand Clapping" and watched it over and over. And when she watched online "The Linda McCartney Story"—a biopic released in 2000—she became obsessed with Linda as well. Linda became her style icon. "She could wear anything and look beautiful. I've always aspired to be able to throw together an outfit like that."

In these modern times, Grace didn't even need to spend her hard-earned money on buying the music. She had an Mp3 player, and whatever CDs they didn't have at home she would burn from the library's collection, then listen to the same songs hundreds of times. As she grew she came to appreciate vinyl and found the format soothing, so much so that she became a collector. She started by adopting her uncle's greatest hits albums that were just lying around and then began buying her own 45s with the Apple label spinning around on them. She currently has lots of Paul McCartney albums solo and with Wings and many John Lennon albums including *Double Fantasy.*

"In any music library, if you're a Beatles person, you have to have some of their individual music. 'Wildlife,' is one of my favorites. It just so beautiful. It's crazy to listen to them all [on vinyl.] You hear the little crackle. That so soothing."

Insightfully, Grace told me what she thinks attracts her generation to the boys.

"In my experience, it was like Christmas morning discovering Beatles music. It's not something a lot of people grow up with, but then you hear it and you're obsessed. For people my age some of it's the music. Some people are really into that. Some people are really into the lyrics, and some people are really into the aesthetics and the novelty of these four boys with cute hair, each with their own personality, each playing a specific role, who go through these style transformations that are so cool. Some of it might be the history. The Beatles are so huge that they're everywhere. I remember people wearing Beatles T-shirts when I was in middle school. I think a lot of people in my age group are infatuated with the past. You'll see a lot of Instagram accounts that are devoted to the '60s and '70s and someone in their 20s is running it. We are obsessed with nostalgia."

Grace knows that The Beatles are beyond nostalgia and are still relevant and important today.

"There are myriad reasons why someone my age should listen to The Beatles. People always say to understand the future you need to understand the past. There's so much influence packed into their music over the span of less than 10 years. The impact they had together was so powerful and so multifaceted. There's something magnetic about a group like that that's still magnetic today. There so much for someone my age to learn in terms of music theory, or songwriting. If they're interested in history there's a lot that The Beatle could teach them."

As Grace grew learning about The Beatles became a wonderful, comforting pastime for her. "It was something you could retreat to when high school was just annoying. It helped me feel less lonely.... Being introverted you need something like that. You can bond with the right people over it too. It goes both ways."

The Beatles' message of love hit Grace right between the eyes. Their lifestyles, especially Paul's, touched and inspired her.

"They were very peace forward," Grace said. "They're outlook is calming and reassuring. I even considered going vegetarian because Paul and Linda were vegetarian."

Grace was affected deeply, albeit in a different way by John and Yoko.

"There are a lot of spicy opinions about John Lennon, but to me he was just on the cusp of really experiencing adulthood without this crazy interference of fame when he died." He was becoming sort of a tamed-down version of himself by becoming domestic. It's cool to see in *Double Fantasy* how much family meant to him at that time. But I also think he was a free thinker ahead of his time, and that's inspiring to me. You think "How would things be now if John Lennon were alive, and honestly I can't think of what kind of personality he would have, what his take would be on current artists, if he and Yoko would still be together, and if there would have been a reunion album. It's all that stuff that lives inside nostalgia forever. But you do always wonder."

Paul's wholesomeness and humility cut Grace to the core, making him her ultimate favorite. "It's so hard to describe. His genius isn't showy. It hits you when you least expect it. When you think of John Lennon, what got him in the news was saying all those radical things, and we love him for that. But Paul McCartney didn't really do that. He has this je ne sais quoi.... I don't feel like any other Beatle could release a record of "Mary Had a Little Lamb" and have it do well. He just has that ability to market anything into a good song."

It's the Beatles' individuality that has kept Grace with them throughout her young life.

"Going back and forth, learning about them, hearing stories that just get released that you would think maybe they would take to their grave, but I'm into it. It hit me that wow, this is some of the best music you're ever going to hear, and you're always going to love it. It could be years since I've listened to a Beatles album, but every time I do, it feels like the first time. Each individual member elicits a different sort of feeling."

Even in Grace's younger years, Paul McCartney's entire catalog was much more interesting to her than pop music of her generation ever was. Once her curiosity was peaked, she wanted to go beyond the music.

"I spent a crazy amount of hours online trying to dig up obscure information. I've done a crazy amount of research. I feel like if you ask me to tell the story of Paul McCartney's whole adulthood, I could probably tell you that. The Beatles were a total obsession for me. When I get into something like that I find out as much information as I can. I'm a night owl and I would stay up until two in the morning, going to school exhausted the next day. Even in college I tried to buy the Linda McCartney *Life in Pictures* book and even cookbooks even though I'm not exclusively vegetarian."

The Beatles, Grace said, "opened my eyes to music I would have overlooked, but I'm so much greater and richer for knowing it. When you think of the Lennon-McCartney songwriting team and then them branching out and doing their own things, imagine the possibilities of that. That's all in their music. . . . I think the huge thing is that [young people] might have an idea that The Beatles are grandparents' music; it's so universal. It'll just take you by surprise."

By the time you read this, Grace and I will have shared her first Paul McCartney concert. I can't wait to hear her reaction when she sees him live for the first time.

Grace wants to share her knowledge and love of the music world by incorporating writing about music into her journalism career. Tomorrow never knows.

He Was Just Eighteen

It was hot and muddy on day two of the annual three-day Firefly Festival, a music fest that could be called a mini-Coachella. The year was 2015, and as it does every year, the event took place in the Woodlands of the Dover Motor Speedway, a 105-acre festival ground in Dover, Delaware. The lineup included Zed, Sublime with Rome, Walk the Moon, and Kid Cudi, bands that I am too old to be familiar with. But the headliner? Paul McCartney!

The festival crowd was young, and the event included camping out in the mud. Nick Favazza, now 25, as well as his girlfriend, Sam Spica, and one of his best friends, Bryan Wehner—who happens to be my son—were there. Nick is a die-hard Paul McCartney fan, and my son had no choice but to grow up to be a fan by association. The tickets for the entire three days were only $200 each; when Nick heard that, he had to go. "I knew there was no way we were ever going to get Paul McCartney tickets that were that good for less than $200. This was our chance to go see him and be there." Bryan and Sam were in.

The festival had multiple stages with different artists from different genres. The crowd bounced easily from one stage to the next. But on the

Bryan Wehner (my son; left) and his best friend, second-generation Beatles fan Nick Favazza, at Fenway Park in Boston before their second Paul McCartney concert together, 2016.

second day when Paul was on the bill, our trio scoped out the big stage that was right in the middle. Nick knew that's where his idol would play. "We decided to just post up there," Nick said. "We stood there for three or four hours just to be a little closer to the stage."

At first there weren't that many people there. But as the night went on and it was just about an hour out, people started to flood the area. "We looked behind us, and there was a good few football fields back of just people. It was crazy! It was really cool!" Most of the attendees were in their late teens and early 20s. Nick and the gang were all 18 and 19 and only 100 feet from the stage!

"It was equivalent to a stadium performance, and we were pretty close. It felt like more people because everyone was standing next to each other, and it was all pretty much in one area."

Despite being born 25 years after The Beatles broke up, everyone definitely knew who Paul McCartney was, Nick said. "Literally, the person before Paul came out was Steve Aoki, who's a big EDM—electronic dance music—DJ. That's where most people were before Paul came out. So, it's funny to see that same crowd transition over to The Beatles basically and know all the words and be into it! It shows that even as music has progressed to literally electronic dance music, people are still enamored by The Beatles. It's crazy."

It wasn't just by chance that the crowd gravitated to Paul. He was

34

the last performance of the night; people could have left if they had their fill, but the majority of people who were there stayed to watch Paul and sing along to every song.

Nick is a lifelong fan, a fandom that started in first grade listening to Beatles music in the car with his grandfather.

Nick couldn't hold it back. When he saw Paul walk onstage, he screamed!

"It was pretty unreal when he walked out. I was like screaming! It was hilarious because I saw Beatlemania [videos of screaming fans], and it was kind of funny or quaint. But it happened to me! I was like *Oh My God! I can't believe this is actually happening! This is all real!* We all cheered when he came out, and I was probably the most excited of the three of us. I was like *Oh My God! This is real life! This is actually happening! It's not just stories that people tell!* It was really cool."

Nick said that he had "been listening to the music all my life. I remember being seriously awestruck by it, and it felt like I was seeing history in a way too. It didn't feel real up until that moment. The Beatles are obviously a cultural thing—a pop culture phenomenon. Their music is so embedded in everything in terms of modern music. It doesn't feel like it actually happened—you just made the assumption that at some point in time this thing happened." Seeing Paul onstage "didn't feel real."

Nick was mesmerized. He didn't want to miss a moment. His eyes were locked on the stage until the iconic moment when Paul led the crowd in audience participation in the Na Na Nas of "Hey Jude."

"It's unbelievable. Even among this younger audience everyone knew all the words, and when there's no words anymore people were really into it. I was looking around during that." After taking it all in, Nick wondered what it must have been like from Paul's vantage point.

"Could you imagine writing something or doing anything and 50-plus years later people are still belting it out or recognizing it?! That must be such a validating feeling. It was incredible to look around and see that everyone was so into it."

Nick's other favorite moment of the night was when Paul played "Something" on the ukulele in honor of George. Again, a moment that stepped out of history into real life.

The following summer Nick's girlfriend Sam surprised him with tickets to see Paul at Fenway Park in Boston. The show was amazing, Paul had great energy, and the crowd—although skewed a bit older— was just as into it. But as in most things in life, there's nothing like the first time. But our young Nick was still impressed. "I remember saying, 'How is this guy at 76 or 77 still belting out three-hour–long concerts full blast night after night?! I remember it being very, very high energy," he said.

"What's that phrase—you can't go home again? I loved it the second time. It was still amazing and great to see. But I think that first time—seeing it all play out and hearing all these songs in real life, played by the person who wrote them—that was surreal. Being in that crowd while everyone was singing along. It's just hard to beat that."

Nick's appreciation of the music began when his grandfather played it in the car and said they were great because they could just scream for three minutes, and it would sound great. This was the early 2000s when bands like Fall Out Boy and Green Day were screaming their hearts out all the time, so little Nick thought his grandpa was funny. His grandpa, who was 19 when the Beatles hit *Ed Sullivan*, told him that's where Nick's favorite bands got it from, but to little Nick that statement didn't register, and it was still funny.

Grown-up Nick, now in medical school, has spent some time on his commute to school listening to The Beatles' contemporaries and realized that The Beatles were indeed unique. What he finds fascinating about their music is that you can't pinpoint their later music, especially starting with *Sgt. Pepper's Lonely Hearts Club Band*, to a particular decade.

"If you go to Johnny Rockets [a '50s-themed restaurant], whatever they're playing on the speakers sounds like it's from the '50s or early '60s, but you can't pin that down with The Beatles."

The early Beatles also hold a special place in Nick's heart. When he started high school, he was a little lonely. His closest friends were districted to another high school on the other side of town. He found himself alone and bereft. Early Beatles music was upbeat and positive. It was a way to escape some of that. He would always listen to it in the morning to get ready for the day, especially "Help" and "Rubber Soul." When he got older and found himself a bit more, he moved on to the later Beatles starting with *Sgt. Pepper*, music that young Nick couldn't relate to.

"I remember listening to it [*Sgt. Pepper*] for the first time when I was younger and thinking *okay, this is weird. Why would anyone listen to this? This is strange.* You'd hear stuff from *Magical Mystery Tour*, and you're like *Okay,—I am The Walrus—good for you, but not my cup of tea.*"

As Nick got older, he read up about The Beatles' changing style and started to understand the transition from live performance to the studio and what they were able to accomplish. At that point he became more interested in listening and trying to discern the changes. Now *Sgt. Pepper* is his favorite Beatles album. He loves the interesting variety of music and realizes that the changes are incredible.

"That's how my listening to The Beatles progressed. I was more drawn in the beginning to those classic standards. 'Hey Jude' and 'Let it Be' were the ones that I first heard and thought *Wow! These guys are really good.* And it went from there."

Like all of our younger fans, Nick is a product of his generation. When he started collecting the music, he wasn't even aware that it all came on albums.

"It all started on iTunes. I would buy songs for 99 cents on the iTunes store on my iPod Touch from back in 2010. The iPod Touch was the big revolutionary thing. You had the fake lighter on there, Doodle Jump [a popular video game] and Beatles records. On mine at least. That's how I started accumulating Beatles albums. I grew up in a time where my family just burned CDs off LimeWire [file-sharing app]. I never had the experience of going to a store and thinking I want this album. So, I never got the concept at that point of *Oh! Songs come on this big disc and there's X tracks.* I didn't really understand the whole concept of what a record was, so I would just buy songs that I liked. It was more piecemeal. And then on top of that when I did figure out that I could just buy all the songs at once on this one album, I was buying anthology albums. It wasn't a very intentional process; it was more *I just don't know how to do this.*"

After Nick bought lots of Beatles songs, his mom pulled out her red and blue album CDs. He sort of got the idea of what records were, but still he downloaded them and put them on his iPod.

Then Nick needed more. In his freshman year of college, he started his vinyl collection. The following summer was when he saw the Firefly concert.

"I'm really interested to know what it would sound like originally and how it was meant to be listened to," Nick said. He's still working on that collection.

As Nick grew, so did his appreciation of the music.

"I enjoyed the classical components that they added. The way they played around with classical instruments along with rock and roll. All this stuff's been said before, but it's true. It always struck me as unique and fun."

Nick listens to all kinds of music and sometimes realizes it's been years since he listened to a Beatles album all the way through. That's when he'll play a classic on Spotify in his car on the way to school. The music is still phenomenal, but it's also like hearing from an old friend.

"It [the music] reminds me of the good times. It makes me think of the concert itself. It makes me think of how the music helped me back in high school. I also reflect back on listening to it with my grandpa in the car. I have a lot of good memories associated with it."

Nick, it's getting better all the time.

Two

I've Just Seen a Tattoo

The first time I heard of a Macca tattoo was from my son Bryan. Fans in the know call Paul McCartney by his nickname, Macca. My son was 19 when he went with Nick Favazza and Sam Spica to the Firefly festival a three-day music extravaganza Paul was headlining. It was incredible that Paul could headline a music festival filled with millennials and Gen Z kids. My son and his friends were able to get way up close to the stage. Why he didn't take his mom is beyond me (just kidding). But can you say "jealous"? Anyway, when he was showing me videos and telling me about this amazing event, he said there was a girl who got onstage, and Paul autographed her arm. She was around my son's age!

I couldn't imagine what you would do with an autograph on your arm; it would wash off. Oh my God, am I really that old that I did not even think of tattooing it? Well, my son filled me in as only a 19-year-old guy can talk to his mom. "She'll get it inked, I guess," he said. Man, what a lucky girl. She was only in her 20s. I'm in my 50s. I've loved Paul McCartney longer than she has. How is that fair? I wanted to scream. I would settle for a hug. Okay, even a handshake would do.

In my journeys to explore resources and to interview people for this book, I came across a Facebook group. I can't tell you the name, because it's a secret, private group. But everyone in this group sports a Macca tattoo somewhere. And they all got to go onstage not only to meet Paul and have him autograph some crazy places on their bodies but, more importantly, to get a hug from him. That hug is my goal in life.

The through line to every one of these stories is that Paul makes you completely comfortable onstage. He makes you feel as if you belong. You are instantly able to talk with him as if he is an old friend. He is a down-to-earth, sweet, humble man.

These interviews were a lot of fun. I felt the excitement as these lucky fans told me their stories.

And hopefully, somehow, these interviews will bring me one step closer to that hug.

When She's 64

A fan finally got her wish in her 60s.

"About time I get f**ing signed!"

That is the sign that made Joy Cohen's dream come true. Paul read it and brought her onstage to finally get the autograph she had been waiting for her entire life.

"I knew when he got to the part [in the concert] where he said, 'I try not to read the signs; I get distracted,' that that's when he's picking [who he will call onstage]," Joy said. "I was sitting in the same row as Nancy [Paul's wife], but before that point, she and her whole entourage got up and left. When I realized they were not coming back, I decided to scoot over. I'm 4'11". He probably never sees me, but since the whole row was empty, that caught his attention."

When Paul's head of security, Brian Riddle, came to bring Joy backstage, she actually thought she was getting tossed out of the show. "Like I said, I'm short. So, for the first time ever, I stood on my chair. I don't ever do that because I'm mindful of the people behind me. Two women behind me kept yelling at me to get down, but it was the first time I could ever see. So when Brian came to get me, I thought I was getting kicked out! That made it so much sweeter!"

Joy Cohen getting Paul's autograph on her arm onstage at Bryce Jordan Center in State College, Pennsylvania, October 15, 2015.

Joy Cohen embracing Paul onstage after she got his autograph, October 15, 2015.

While waiting in the wings, Joy was nervous and thought she was going to die. But she realized nerves would make her miss her moments with Paul. She walked onstage ready for anything.

"There's something about him that puts you at ease," she said. "I was arguing with him. That's how comfortable I was." "Arguing" is a strong word for the banter she and Paul shared. "I wanted my sign to say "Please" and ""Thank you," but there wasn't enough room, and I couldn't squeeze it in. So it just said, "Please and Thank." You think no one will ever notice. But guess who noticed and pointed it out to 40,000 other people? I tried to explain to him that I ran out of room! Everyone laughed, and I got a hug! I know exactly what I did at that moment. I looked upward and said, "Mom, look what I'm doing." I know she would have been thrilled. It's over before you know it. But now I know miracles do happen. That kind of stuff happens to other people. It doesn't happen to me."

Joy's autograph and subsequent tattoo is on her right forearm just below the elbow. "Most girls do it on their shoulder to hide it at work," Joy said. "I'm retired. I wanted to be able to see it whenever I want. If I can't see it, it didn't happen!"

Paul showing Joy's arm to audience, October 15, 2015—What's a guy to do?

Luck seemed to follow Joy her entire life. In 1965 when she was 14, she won a ticket to see The Beatles at Shea Stadium. WIBG radio in Philadelphia, where Joy still lives, held a contest where 99 lucky winners (the station was 99 on the FM dial) got a ticket to Shea, including transportation on a coach bus. Fans were told to mail in postcards with their names and phone numbers. At that time it was a penny a postcard. Joy sent 25 postcards, costing her 25 cents, a big investment in her teenage life. Contestants had 10 minutes to call back if the DJ called their name. Then they were on they were on their way to Shea.

"The first winner was called. It wasn't me," Joy said. "I was moping around the house. Second, not me. The third winner, wait ... that's me! None of us could remember the phone number, my mother, my brother.... Thank God we had someone else in the house that day who had no stake in any of this. She remembered, and she dialed the phone. Then my friend won too!"

On the day of the concert, three buses left Philadelphia headed to New York. Joy felt like she was going to camp until they got off the buses at Shea Stadium and saw the crowds of girls.

The contest winners squeezed their way through the cheering crowd and climbed the stairs to the seats. "They weren't the best seats, but I was there!" Joy said. "You couldn't hear anything ... just screaming. I was proudly one of the screamers. That was part of the fun too!"

Joy saw The Beatles two more times in Philly. She has been to every

US McCartney tour since the '70s. And now her mission is to turn her two-year-old granddaughter into a fan. She's taking her to see a tribute band soon. Maybe I'll be writing about her in 20 years.

Why Don't We Do It in the Road

This fan got her autograph on the side of the road!
(In Trish Peterson's own words)

My sister Carolyn is an original Beatles fan. Her favorite Beatle was always "the cute one," Paul McCartney. She was one of the screaming young teenage girls at their performance during the Indiana State Fair on September 3, 1964. Three days later on September 6, our baby sister was born. Carolyn was such a big fan of the Beatles that she somehow talked my mother into naming our baby sister Cynthia, after Cynthia Lennon, John's first wife. Not only has Carolyn seen Paul perform live as a Beatle, but she has also seen him in concert with Wings and most

Trish Peterson getting Paul McCartney's autograph on the side of the road before he takes off to do a concert. Outside Great American Ballpark, Cincinnati, Ohio, August 4, 2011.

recently as a solo performer. I grew up hearing Beatles music being played on vinyl records and albums by her and my older brother. So naturally, I soon was a young Beatles fan too. Fast-forward to 2018. All told, we have probably been to 15 states and have now seen Paul McCartney perform in concert nearly 50 times. We have experienced several memorable "Paul Encounters" along the way. Our MO is to arrive very early to each venue in order to be in prime position for what is known as the "Limo Watch."

Trish Peterson's tattoo, 2011.

August 4, 2011, my sister and I once again had concert tickets to see Paul McCartney. This time he would be playing at Great American Ballpark in Cincinnati, Ohio, a mere three-hour drive from our hometown in central Indiana—relatively close by our standards. We agreed that I would pick her up at noon, but I arrived 10 minutes late because she is never ready on time. And she wasn't. I waited around 30 minutes before she finally came out and got in the car. We fussed at each other the entire drive to Cincinnati, each blaming the other for being late. This tardiness could ruin our whole plan to be in place in time for the Limo Watch.

We get within eyesight of the stadium, to the left of the interstate, but miss our exit and end up over the river into Kentucky. Tempers flare, each still blaming the other. More precious time ticks away, but we finally make our way back to the stadium. As per our normal routine, we "case the joint" in order to ascertain the logistics and layout of the venue and best determine probable route of arrival. That way we can then get in to prime position for the Limo Watch.

We make our first pass around the stadium and immediately notice "Paul personnel" (head of security, official photographer, etc.) in the vicinity. This normally only occurs when Paul's arrival is imminent. "Uh oh!" How can this be? We have arrived about two hours earlier than standard. It's not time for Paul to arrive yet! We are stopped at a red light, a block behind the stadium, when we hear sirens. "Oh no!" It can't be! (Paul always arrives with a police-escorted entourage, sirens blaring.) "Let's hope this is a funeral procession!" Zip! Zip! Zip! Zip! Four black SUVs escorted by two police cars zip through the intersection right in front of us. It was HIM!!! We are both instantly mad. We missed it! We missed Paul's arrival. We missed it! Now the fight begins in earnest. She's mad at me; I'm mad at her. She's yelling at me, "It's all your fault!" I'm yelling at her, "It's all YOUR fault!" Finally the light turns green, and we take a left back toward the stadium.

We approach the next intersection, and the light is red. We come up behind an old Ford Bronco. Just then, the driver jumps out, opens the back door, and pulls out a small toddler. "What's going on?" He runs away from the vehicle with the toddler dangling from his arms. The light

07·25·2010 20:23

Trish Peterson's Paul onstage closeup from the fourth row, August 4, 2011.

changes to green, but the Bronco doesn't move. No one is in the vehicle. We back up and pull around the Bronco. We look to the left and see the driver with the toddler. Just then I notice HIM. It's him, it's him! It's Paul McCartney standing right there on the sidewalk behind the stadium. I jump out of the moving car right in the middle of the street to run over to Paul. As I do, the man with the toddler is now to my left. Another gentleman is running up the sidewalk to my right. My thought is "no one will ever believe this!" As we approach Paul, I ask each gentleman, "Do you have a pen?" "No." "Do you have a pen?" "No." Crap! No one will ever believe this! Wouldn't you know, I jumped out of the car without any paper or pen or anything! We were always ready with items needed to obtain an autograph, and it was all in the car! Oh well, no one will ever believe this, but I'll know! Then as luck would have it, I notice that Paul has a sharpie marker! When he arrived at the stadium, Paul McCartney had gotten out of his SUV and greeted the few fans who were there waiting. This never happens!!! (There were only a few fans present because of his earlier than usual arrival.) I said hello to Paul, stuck out my arm and said "Paul, I need a tattoo!" I didn't know what else to do. I didn't have anything for him to autograph except me! "Well then!" he said. "What will your husband say about this?" "Who???," I replied. We both chuckled. He rolled up the right sleeve of my yellow Elvis T-shirt and very carefully drew his signature onto my arm. "There! How's that?" I couldn't even speak. I stared into his eyes and muttered "thank you." "I have to go now," he said to us and disappeared into the tunnel of the stadium.

I was on cloud nine. I called everyone I knew to tell them I had just been autographed by Paul McCartney!! Still, somehow I felt like no one would believe this really happened. Several hours later as I approached the front of the stadium to enter for the concert, just by chance a news reporter, and her cameraman stopped me. I told her about my encounter with Paul and showed her my autograph. At the concert that night, I was showing off my autograph to some other nearby fans. Everyone was very happy for me and congratulating me. Shortly thereafter, the gal next to me spilled beer on me. She did it a second time, and I realized she was jealous of my Paul McCartney signature and trying to ruin the autograph. That didn't go over well, to say the least! My sister wanted to fight her if she did it again. Luckily, the instigator departed.

The next day the short interview appeared on the local TV news channel and in the newspaper. I even found the story on the internet. After the beer incident, I decided to place a section of clear packing tape over the autograph to protect it. A few days later, I had the signature tattooed onto my right shoulder blade. I pulled off the packing tape, and the signature had transferred to the tape. I promptly framed the tape. About a week later, I get a "friend request" on Facebook from someone I don't know. I notice it is someone from Cincinnati. I go ahead and accept the request. I can always block it if it turns out to be some scammer, right? Well, it turns out this person was there when Paul signed me, and she took a picture. She didn't know who I was until she saw me on the news and read my name and hometown in the newspaper. She tracked me down on Facebook and asked me if I would like to have the picture of Paul McCartney autographing my arm? Of course! In the end, the encounter that I worried no one would ever believe is documented on the television news, printed in the local newspaper, posted on the internet, and tattooed on my body, and I even have an actual photograph of that special moment when I met Paul McCartney!

My Brave Foot

He signed the "ugliest foot in the world."

Cancer patients light up when they see Nina Galpern's left foot. Why? It's got Paul's autograph tattooed on top. When she wears her ballet flats, this cancer center health educator gets lots of questions about how she got it. And she loves telling the story. Her story tells of serendipity. It tells of taking a leap of faith. And it tells how serendipity made a lifelong dream come true.

The concert was in Greensboro, North Carolina, on October 30, 2014. It was an unexpected appearance. Paul McCartney's original tour schedule did not include Greensboro, but because he had been sick in the spring, the whole schedule was shuffled around, and Greensboro was added at the last minute.

"This show didn't even exist!" Nina said. "I was sitting on a train coming back from visiting my daughter in Boston. I wasn't planning on going to Greensboro, but I thought I'd look for a ticket anyway. The first ticket that came up was bad. I checked again. Then one came up in the second row on the floor near the center. I said, 'There's got to be a reason that came up. I guess I'm going to Greensboro.'"

On October 29, 2014, the day before the show, Nina got a ticket to ride and boarded a train to Greensboro with her friends. She traditionally brings signs to Paul's concerts, hoping he'll notice her. She got to work on her sign on the 10-hour ride.

Nina Galpern living the dream onstage with Paul and her sign "Trick or Treat, please sign my feet," in Greensboro, North Carolina, on October 30, 2014.

"The show was the night before Halloween, so I had to go with the theme," she said. "I wrote, 'Trick or Treat, please sign my feet.' I thought it was the silliest sign ever. I did it as kind of a joke. I always brought a sign, but I never asked to be signed before. My signs always said something to him—'You're Brilliant'—but I never asked to be signed because I didn't really want a tattoo. In fact, in 2009 in Boston I had a sign that said 'No tattoo, a kiss will do.' He read it out loud, and it got on the big screen at Fenway. A couple of people told me his security guard came over to get me, and at the last second they didn't bring me up."

But life is what happens when you're busy making other plans. If Nina had gotten onstage in Boston, it probably would not have happened in Greensboro.

When the train pulled into the Greensboro station, Nina looked down at her open-toed shoes and realized she needed a pedicure—stat. If she actually got onstage, those would not be the tootsies she wanted to show off. She did not have time for the professional kind, so she ran to the mall, got bright red nail polish, and did a quick paint job. She said she did a horrendous job and never dreamed her feet would end up all over the internet. The pedicure was so bad, in fact, that when her toes became famous, some people posted that hers was the ugliest foot in the universe.

But her idol did not even notice. "He read the sign early in the show," she said. "I was so excited that he actually read it that I put it away. I thought that was the end of it."

It wasn't. Later in the show Paul sent his security guard, Brian Riddle, to find Nina. People saw him walk up and down the aisles. Since she had put her sign away, she was lost in the crowd. The Brian signaled Paul, letting him know his dilemma. "That's when Paul said onstage, 'Someone over here had a sign about getting her foot signed. You might just get your wish.'"

What's a girl supposed to do? Nina started screaming and held her sign over her head. Brian ran to her and said, "You're going up!" He escorted her backstage, where she noticed a very curious prop: Brian was holding a pile of white towels. He told her to take off her sneakers. That's when her nerves kicked in. *This is really happening*, she thought.

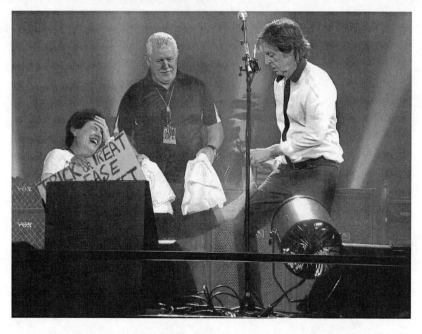

Nina Galpern laughing hysterically—can this really be happening?—while she puts her bare foot on Paul's thigh! October 30, 2014.

I can't believe this is really happening. "I really thought he was going to sign my shoe."

Nina was escorted backstage barefoot to the opposite side of the stage, where she was told to put her shoes back on. Then it happened. She was escorted onstage with her shoes on, and time stood still. Nina tells the story:

"It was like everything was in slow motion. I was only up there three and a half minutes, but it felt like hours. They brought me up, and all of a sudden a chair appeared. [Paul] asked me what my name was. That's the only word I said the whole time. At first I thought he was gonna sign my shoe, and he said, 'Nope. If we're gonna do this, we're gonna do it right.' So I literally had to grab onto him because I couldn't balance. I was gonna fall. I held onto him for I don't know how long to take my shoes off. I didn't know which foot he was gonna sign, so I took them both off. I was sitting with these horrible toes. It was really bad."

"They stuck me in this chair. Meanwhile, Brian Riddle had a stack of towels. He also had a can of spray Odor Eaters. It was hysterical because Paul starts making all these comments. 'This is a first ... and last.' He's making it really funny, and he takes my foot—I was sitting

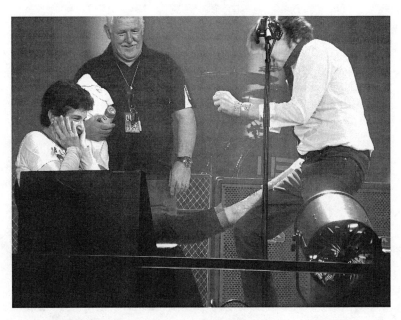

Nina Galpern's bare left foot—way up Paul's McCartney's thigh on stage, October 30, 2014.

Nina getting that Paul McCartney hug, October 30, 2014.

on a chair—he holds me by the ankle and plops it right on his upper thigh. Literally. It was pretty high up. I'm like covering my face. I can't believe it—laughing hysterically. The audience is laughing hysterically. The camera zoomed in. The next thing you know, I didn't have a Sharpie. I didn't have anything. Luckily, his assistant had a Sharpie. I was sitting with these horrible toes. It was really bad."

"Before he signed it, he took the can of Odor Eaters, and he sprayed it on my foot. Like a knee-jerk reaction, my foot went up, and I thought I kicked him. I'm thinking *Oh my God, I just kicked him.* And that would have been the end of him and me, and I would have been arrested. It went up as a reflex because it tickled. Paul's wiping it with a towel. He's making a big production of it, and then he signs it, and then I stood up."

"He signed it and did a little underline. I gave him a big hug, and then the funniest line came. Brian escorted me off the stage, and Paul says, 'I used to be a serious rock and roll man till Nina came along!'"

"When you're onstage, you go into slow motion. It seems like it's not a real experience. After 50 years, finally my foot is sitting on his leg. None of it made any sense."

In the lobby, Nina was still wearing only one shoe; she couldn't smudge her small miracle. People took pictures of her foot. It was later headlined on a website and called "The Ugliest Foot on Earth." "That may be," Nina said. "But it's got Paul's autograph. Who else can say that?"

Nina wasn't sure what she was going to do. Still not thinking of a tattoo, she ran into a man on the way home who had been on the train on the way there. He'd been at the show and recognized her. He was covered in tattoos and told Nina she would regret it if she didn't get it tattooed. He even recommended his favorite shop.

Nina called her husband, and he told her she couldn't get buried in a Jewish cemetery if she got the tattoo. So she spent her time on the train calling the manager of a cemetery. Turns out, that's an old wives' tale. Forty-eight hours later, she had the tattoo.

"I'm still telling the story," Nina said. "It's bringing joy to other people, and I like that. It keeps paying it forward. I have always loved him so much. To have something like this is a treasure."

Put It There

Mom and daughter get autographs in the exact same place.

"His hands were soft and his eyes...." I promised Sharon I would not make her sound like a lovesick teen, but maybe it's the teenybopper in me that made me start her story this way. His soft hands and deep eyes are what Sharon White of the San Francisco Bay Area remembers about being onstage with her idol.

Sharon has been a Beatles fan as long as she can remember. She can pinpoint her start to when she was four years old and her aunt gave her parents some Beatles albums. Her parents weren't interested. But Sharon went to bed every night with the lads singing to her softly. Paul was immediately her favorite. Now in her mid–50s, she shared her surreal onstage moment with her just-as-lovestruck daughter, who is now 24.

At this point in the chapter, the story may be starting to sound familiar. But each family—each person—has its own unique twist. Sharon's onstage story in itself is amazing. But the fact that it's not the only time she has met the man himself and that she has been on TV (*The Ellen DeGeneres Show* and *Entertainment Tonight*) because her love for Paul makes her story that much more drool-worthy.

In high school, Sharon was known as the girl who loved Paul at a

Sharon White and her daughter Laurel onstage with Paul just before he autographs them both on the upper right shoulder in Missoula, Montana, August 2014.

time when you were an oddball to be a Beatles fan. It was the 1970s, and kids were listening to Michael Jackson and Donna Summer. They would actually pose the question "Paul McCartney was in another band before Wings?" Still, she wore her fandom on her sleeve.

All her loving paid off in August 2014 in Missoula, Montana. Sharon and her daughter, Laurel, had the VIP sound check package. That means they were two of the select few who got to see Paul and his full band rehearse for about an hour before the show. During rehearsal Paul plays whatever comes to mind, not following any set list. Sharon was blown away when the band played "Hope of Deliverance." She hadn't heard it live for decades, and it was the first time Laurel had ever heard it live. As my people say at Passover, if that were all that had taken place, "it would have been sufficient."

But a lot more was to come that night. Sharon and Laurel held up their homemade signs during the sound check, knowing there was a chance they would be the chosen ones called onstage. Sharon's sign said "You're the only tattoo I approve of for my daughter." Laurel's read "I'm the daughter. Please sign me!"

A few hours after sound check was over, Sharon and Laurel were dancing during the actual concert. That's when Paul's head security guard, Brian Riddle, came over to their seats. "He told us to follow him. It was absolutely surreal," Sharon said. Next thing you know they were in the wings, dancing with Brian and waiting to go onstage. "We were so excited that we didn't bring our signs with us." Paul remembered what the signs said. Sharon tells the story:

> Onstage, Paul asked me, "Are you sure you approve?"
> I said, "Yes, and I want one too."
> The audience laughed. He asked us where we wanted him to sign. We pointed to the exact same place at the exact same time. The audience laughed again. We got his autograph on our upper back/right shoulder. He signed us both. We each got a couple of hugs and a kiss on the cheek.

Laurel and Sharon White with their freshly minted Paul McCartney tattoos on their upper right shoulders, 2014.

While she was standing onstage with Paul, all Sharon could think was "I was standing there with Paul McCartney. It was unreal. Most people talk about his smell, but I didn't notice that." Sharon wasn't nervous being onstage, just excited. She says she was thinking "This is someone who I have looked up to as long as I can remember. He's the only person, outside of my family that I wanted to meet and talk to. He's someone I admire so much."

Sharon says Laurel feels the same way about Paul. "When I ask her what she loves about Paul McCartney, she says, 'He's cute, funny, an activist, and a vegetarian.'" Laurel became a vegetarian in seventh grade because of what she learned from Paul and Linda, even though Linda was gone. Laurel admires him for his lifestyle and the choices he has made. "And here's Paul McCartney," says Sharon, "and we get a moment together with him. It was such an exciting moment and so great to be able to have that with my daughter."

But wait, there's more. This was not Sharon's first brush with "the cute one." That would be in 2005 when he did a book signing in Los Angeles for *High in the Clouds*, a children's adventure novel that Paul cowrote. "It was the four of us. My kids were young at the time. Laurel was ten, and my son was 7. I met him briefly there. I shook his hand twice just so I could stay there and be with him a second or two longer."

Sharon tells this story casually, leaving out the fact that on that same day a few hours later she appeared on *Ellen* in the front row, chosen by Ellen's producers to ask Paul a question while he was a guest on the show. Sharon found out through a friend on a Paul McCartney message board that the *Ellen* show had asked people to submit questions they would ask Paul, with the chance they would be chosen to be on the show. Sharon doesn't remember the question she submitted, but she sent it along with a photo that she had captured from Paul McCartney's website. In it, she was in the front row at a concert in Phoenix holding a "goofy sign" over her head. It took a little cajoling, but finally Sharon revealed what the sign said: "Sharon loves Paul" with a heart in the middle.

A few months later, Sharon got a call from one of the *Ellen* producers inviting her on the show. Coincidentally, the taping was the same day as the book signing. While they were waiting in line for *Ellen*, who comes out but Ellen herself asking for Sharon White. Sharon's response when Ellen asked her why she loves Paul? "He's the cute one!" she said. Why not go for the cliché?

Production assistants put Sharon's husband and kids in a conference room where they could watch the taping on a monitor because the kids were too young to go into the studio. Sharon was given a seat in the audience in the front row. They put a mic on her, then handed her a different question from the one she had submitted. Sharon was seated next to another woman who had actually seen The Beatles at the Hollywood Bowl. She too was assigned a question. The two practiced their lines.

"My assigned question was something like 'I heard that Heather thought that John wrote "Get Back," but actually you wrote it. What do you think?'" Sharon said. "That was not a question I would ever ask, and it was too bad they were having me ask that."

It turned out they didn't have time in the segment, so Ellen ended up asking the questions very quickly. "But when he came onstage, he recognized me from the book signing! He gave me a double finger point, and I did it back to him. For a few shows after that, he recognized me," Sharon said casually, as if it happens to everyone. "There was about a monthlong time in 2005 where he recognized me. It was cool for me, but that doesn't mean there was something unique or special about me." Paul recognizes groups of fans regularly. Many have been to over 100 shows. "He knows them well as someone in the audience and invites them onstage to dance with him."

If you were watching *Entertainment Tonight* in 1993, you might have seen Sharon dancing at a Paul concert. She was in the seventh row in Anaheim. She was the only person as far as she could see on her feet and dancing. She didn't see any cameras in her area, but the next day she was watching *Entertainment Tonight*, a show she had interned on in her college days, "and there I was. Mary Hart had gone to the show, and in the segment, they showed me dancing!"

That was Sharon's first 15 minutes of Paul-related fame. Remember those people back in high school who had made her feel like an oddball for loving Paul? Well, guess who was contacting her now to say they'd seen her on TV?

"Paul's always been my favorite from day one!" There is nothing like your first love.

She Heard the News Today—Oh Boy

Katherine Chipps's first memory is hearing the news that John Lennon had been shot. She was two and a half years old.

"My dad was putting up the Christmas tree when they broke in the news and said that John Lennon was shot," she said. "He just sat down. He was very upset. I remember sitting there watching TV with him. It was incredible."

As a young toddler, she already knew who John Lennon was. That's how important The Beatles have been in her life as well as her father's. John's murder was a huge shock to her and her dad, as it was for everyone. But their love for The Beatles lives on. In fact, one of her dad's bucket list items was to see Paul perform "Blackbird" live.

Almost 40 years later, Katherine purchased tickets for the two of them to see Paul McCartney in 2017 in Detroit, Michigan, as a thank-you to her father for helping her through her divorce.

"He was always jealous of the trips that I've been on to see [Paul],"

Katherine Chipps thanks her dad for all his help by bringing him onstage with Paul McCartney, Detroit, Michigan, 2017 (photo credit Ricky Glover).

Katherine said. "There was one caveat to the ticket; he had to hold up a funny sign."

He had no qualms with that.

"My sign said 'Please sign me—Dad approves.' And my dad's sign said 'Sign my daughter.'"

And then, a miracle.

"I was the luckiest person on the planet that day. They came and got us and said that Paul had chosen us to go onstage! I still can't believe it happened!"

Paul's people came to get Katherine and her dad while Paul was singing "Yesterday." While they waited in the wings Paul played "Day Tripper." Have you ever asked yourself what you would be thinking while you were waiting in the wings to get onstage and meet the man himself? For Katherine, it was her purse.

"I was so nervous I forgot my purse. I had to go back and they kept telling me I had to hurry. Backstage I was so nervous—then I'm like, 'Oh my God.' And I kept thinking, 'Who's going to watch my purse?' But everyone backstage were supernice. A security guard said he would watch it. Then another person with the tour asked me if he could take my camera and take pictures in the front!"

Purse taken care of, her nerves set in.

"I was just trying to keep calm. I kept looking at my dad, like 'This is really happening! This is really happening!'" Then they were out there— in front of 20,000 people—but most importantly standing next to the Paul McCartney.

Katherine recalled that Paul "asked our names. The concert was in Detroit, Michigan, and I'm from Columbus, Ohio. When I said that there were 20,000 boos. We all started laughing and stuff and that kind of broke the ice. After that I was okay. I wasn't as nervous after that point, and Paul made a joke. My dad lives in Toledo, so he said he was a Tigers and Red Wings fan. They all cheered. We just tried to have fun with it."

Then the real magic happened.

"Paul signed my left forearm. I just kept thanking him while he was signing. On my right wrist I have 'Let it Be' tattooed. I showed him that. I was like 'Now my arms match.' He kind of chuckled from that. I mean you're really up there for about two minutes, but it seems like an eternity afterwards."

Seeing Paul's shows has been an expensive habit for Katherine for a long time. When he played in Columbus two years earlier, she sold her motorcycle just so she could get third-row center. After that she started a savings account for show tickets, usually costing her around $1,000 each.

There was a time when Katherine didn't have that kind of money. But good luck seems to follow her at every Macca concert she attends. She had nosebleed seats for a show in 2005. When she and her former husband were getting on the elevator to go up to their seats, someone stopped them. He was from the tour and randomly upgraded them to the 10th row! Katherine flipped out.

It might be that good deed that makes Katherine want to pay it forward. With her Macca tattoo proudly displayed on her left forearm, people often ask if they can touch it. "One person sat and rubbed it for a few minutes while they asked questions about it. I love sharing the experience!"

Katherine shares the common consensus among people who have met the legend.

"Paul was very calming onstage," she said. "He has no ego about him at all. I love being able to share that with people. A lot of times people think of big celebrities with big egos and not really caring about their fans. I think there's a small group of us that have been trying to get onstage forever. It shows that he cares. He knows we're out here."

Paul's calming effect is what makes his fans able to stand in front of tens of thousands of people and not feel the least bit nervous.

"It was a very weird feeling," Katherine said. "At first you have that thought, 'I'm going to be in front of all these people,' and then you get up there and that's the last thing you even think of. Even when they're booing you. I wasn't concerned about the audience."

In case I left you wondering, Paul did sing "Blackbird," and her Katherine's dad, well maybe he was amazed.

THREE

And Now for Something Completely Different

Even the Monty Python gang was touched by The Beatles. George Harrison cofounded Handmade Films to fund the film *Monty Python's Life of Brian* as well as Terry Gilliam's *Time Bandits* and many more.

What else have The Beatles inspired? It is impossible to talk about everything and everyone inspired by the Fab Four, but this chapter will let you in on some little-known events, productions, and businesses that have all sprung up directly or indirectly because of the four lads from Liverpool. There is the tiny town in Arkansas that the boys saved. There are Broadway productions and television shows based on the band. There are businesses, schools, and tour guides that owe their entire business to The Beatles.

This chapter was amazing and enlightening to research. I hope you enjoy learning about these people as much as I did.

In the Town Where They Changed Planes

Walnut Ridge, Arkansas, out of the red and into the black.

There once was a small town in Arkansas in dire straits and close to bankruptcy, complete with derelict buildings on Main Street and town employees not getting paid. It might not have been the town where they were born, but who else could save a town like that? It was a long and winding road, but in the end it was The Beatles who forced the town to come together. Okay, I can hear you groaning.

It was 2010 when the Walnut Ridge Chamber of Commerce met to discuss a marketing plan to raise the town out of its decline. The members were tossing ideas around when a metal sculptor cried out, "The Beatles landed here in 1964." Wait ... what?

And that is how it all began.

Charles Snapp, current mayor of Walnut Ridge, loves to regale people with the story of how The Beatles put this little town in the flatlands of Arkansas on the map. That day turned into a marketing plan that took a depressed town and turned it into a thriving destination. Charles's midwestern twang and his sharp memory for detail makes you feel like a fly on the wall.

The day The Beatles changed planes in Walnut Ridge, Arkansas, September 1964. Ringo is walking to the plane (photograph courtesy Carrie Mae Snapp).

"It was a Friday night, really the wee hours of Saturday morning," Charles said, lost in the memory of the day The Beatles landed when he was just 10 years old. "A Dairy Barn worker was out sweeping the parking lot. He saw a large plane in slow flight with landing lights on. He knew this was uncommon." The airport was an army airfield training base that was not known for nighttime landings. "He told the owner, and the owner called the police. At the same time, there were three college freshmen driving by. They decided to see what was up at the airport. Just as they pulled up to the plane, here come The Beatles exiting the plane! It kind of freaked them out."

Charles learned later that Beatles manager Brian Epstein had decided they would land at that remote airfield, which is the second-largest airport in Arkansas, in the middle of the band's first American tour. Then they would change planes on their way to Alton, Missouri, where they would take a secret break from the mania and rest at a dude ranch.

Back in the day, Charles's sister was a "Beatles junkie" and president

of the local fan club, Beatles Forevermore. One of
those three freshmen who
saw The Beatles lived next
door and called her right
away. She went crazy and
got on the phone to spread
the news to all her fan club
friends. Their mother also
told everyone she knew
until word got to a local
reporter. At that point,
the whole town was dying
to catch a glimpse of The
Beatles.

The Fab Four had to
come back through Wal-
nut Ridge and change
planes again to get on the
next leg of their American
tour. Their landing was set
for a Sunday morning. In
Walnut Ridge, the thing
to do on Sunday morning
is go to church. But people
knew they could get a pass
just this once. "That day,
my parents got me from
a friend's house," Charles
said. "We were building
a fort. They made me get
cleaned up and go to the
airport. I didn't even want
to go! I was ten years old,
5 years younger than my
sister."

John walking between planes in Walnut
Ridge, September 1964 (photograph courtesy Carrie Mae Snapp).

At age ten, Charles
was more in awe of the
crowd size than The Beat-
les. There were about 300

George getting out of a car ready to board
a plane in Walnut Ridge, September 1964
(photograph courtesy Carrie Mae Snapp).

John on the steps of the plane in Walnut Ridge, September 1964 (photograph courtesy Carrie Mae Snapp).

people there, and for a town like Walnut Ridge, that was the size of a Thanksgiving Day football crowd. Town dignitaries were included in the lineup. The sheriff, the police chief, and the mayor were all in attendance for this illustrious event.

"The mayor stood up on the hood of his car," Charles said. "He told the crowd, 'When the boys arrive, we're not gonna mob them. We're gonna stay in an orderly fashion. We'll let them put their stuff on the plane.'" Much to Charles's surprise, the crowd behaved themselves.

A red and white GMC Suburban pulled up behind the crowd, then pulled right up to the steps of the plane. "We had to scoot over to get out of the way," Charles said. "George and Paul were in the red Suburban. John and Ringo were on the plane."

Charles's father took some pictures with his Brownie Instamatic, photos Charles's sister still treasures. A doctor in the crowd took movies on his 8mm movie camera, but the footage did not withstand the test of time.

"The plane was really impressive. It was a DC-10 Electra," Charles said. "So, the guys [George and Paul] load the plane. We tried to get 'em to come off, and they won't come off. The mayor took his daughter's albums on the plane and got autographs. No one else got autographs. It was orderly," said Charles. "Then the plane took off. And that was about the extent of that day. It's one of those weird stories that's been told a thousand times."

Cut to Walnut Ridge Chamber of Commerce meeting, 2010.

When metalworker Denny West mentioned the landing, the proverbial light bulb went on in Charles's head. Not yet mayor, he was a retired business owner and wanted to see the town thrive. He had never thought of connecting the landing to a marketing plan until that moment.

The towns above and below Walnut Ridge already had festivals based on the area's rockabilly history. Early rock legends who took mountain music and blended it with gospel from the cotton fields used to play throughout the area. Many were from northeast Arkansas. The chamber's original thought was to build a "rock and roll highway" out of the town's Main Street and have another festival. But Charles wanted to go beyond a festival. He wanted to build attractions that people would come see on a regular basis. For heaven's sake, they had The Beatles.

Charles set Denny to work. He sculpted a five-foot-wide, two-foot-tall model of the *Abbey Road* album cover in metal. "I saw it," Charles said. "I looked at my wife, Jackie, and I said, 'I can sell this idea to the world.'" The chamber immediately started a fundraising effort for the metal needed to make a 10-foot-tall, 20-foot-wide sculpture.

John carrying a suitcase to the plane with the crowd behind him in Walnut Ridge, September 1964 (photograph courtesy Carrie Mae Snapp).

64

Ringo a few paces in front of John walking to the plane in Walnut Ridge, September 1964 (photograph courtesy Carrie Mae Snapp).

The Liverpool Legends playing at Abbey Road on the River in 2018 to commemorate the day The Beatles changed planes at Walnut Ridge in September 1964.

Beatles Park at Walnut Ridge, 2018.

It was time for the unveiling to the chamber. The local ABC-TV affiliate covered the event, but still there were a lot of naysayers. That didn't deter Charles and his team. ABC picked up the newsclip and used it for a filler around the country because it had The Beatles in it. George Harrison's late sister, Louise, who managed a Beatles tribute band called the Liverpool Legends, saw it in her home of Springfield, Missouri. Three days later she called Charles and told him she wanted to get involved. Right there, Charles knew he was onto something big. He took the scale model and showed it to Louise and the band members. They offered to put on a concert for the public opening. Charles jumped at the opportunity.

Denny, remember Denny, the one who mentioned The Beatles landing at the first chamber meeting? Denny began working on carving the metal sculpture. It took 500 hours. The public unveiling was set for the third Sunday of September 2011, the anniversary of the historic day in 1964 when The Beatles changed planes in Walnut Ridge.

"We put the word out, and there was somewhat of a media frenzy," Charles said, the excitement building in his voice. "Then the *Wall Street Journal* reaches out, and they fly a man out to cover it!"

But the day of the unveiling, it was raining so hard that the local firefighters had to help tarp down the stage so the Liverpool Legends could play.

Walnut Ridge native Sonny Burgess, a recording artist at Sun Studios—known as the birthplace of rock and roll in Memphis, Tennessee—was coming back into town that day. He told Charles, "Snapp, I'm gonna tell you you've got something here. You're gonna want to take this to the next level." Charles didn't follow the logic and asked Sonny what he was talking about. "It's pouring down raining," Sonny told him. "I didn't expect you to have 50 people here, much less 100, but you've got 3,000 or more in raincoats and umbrellas wanting to see you pull the covers off this giant."

The notoriety continued to spread. "Now when you go to downtown Walnut Ridge, you see people you've never seen before from other countries and other states there to get their picture taken down at Beatles Park," Charles said. Charles and the rest of the chamber couldn't let it end there. They started The Beatles at the Ridge festival featuring tribute bands, Beatles experts and authors, symposiums, and lots of memorabilia.

Today, the festival attracts about 10,000 people a year and is always held on the third Saturday of September, the anniversary of the famous landing. In 2017 it was named the top festival in the state. It placed fourth on the top 10 list of places for Beatles history in *USA Today*. "This gave the people of Walnut Ridge a sense of accomplishment," Charles said. "Volunteerism started picking up. At that point I said, 'I think I'm gonna run for mayor. I think we can spread this into every aspect of the community.'"

This town of 5,400 has gotten so much attention that 18 new businesses have sprung up in the last four years. "We have two new restaurants, a new convenience store, a tractor-trailer supply store, a Taco Bell, and a Dollar Store," Charles boasted. The town is as healthy as it has ever been, with sales tax up 26.5 percent and going up 3-10 percent a year. Building permits have skyrocketed. And what's more, there are no more derelict buildings.

"People say they wish they had our marketing ability," Charles said. "It's not our marketing ability. It's the marketing ability of The Beatles. That's an unbelievable powerhouse. You think about it, we appeal to people of all ages. There are kids that grow up and still to this day enjoy Beatles music. It's been an unbelievable ride! It's all because of our willingness to believe in the four lads from Liverpool."

Brian Epstein Posthumously Inspired a Broadway Producer's Life

From page to screen.

"You're crazy! People like you don't do things like that!" That's what Beatles manager Brian Epstein's family and others told him when Epstein said he wanted to manage The Beatles. He was supposed to go into his family's successful furniture business. It's also what Vivek J. Tiwary—Tony Award–winning creative producer of the Broadway smash hit *Jagged Little Pill*, author of the *New York Times* best seller *The Fifth Beatle*, and executive producer of the television show based on the book—was told when he was growing up and said he wanted a life in the arts.

Vivek is a first-generation American of Indian descent. "Young people of Indian origin with some means are expected to pursue engineering or medicine," Vivek said. "They're supposed to become a doctor or lawyer or something in technology. I wasn't supposed to go into the arts, especially without knowing anyone in Bollywood."

Brian Epstein died of an accidental overdose in August 1967. There was not much written about him, and Vivek wanted to know more. As soon as he started researching Brian's life, Vivek felt a connection to him. "There's a direct line between Brian's story and mine," he said. "Brian's story greatly influenced my dreams. The Beatles, part and parcel, were a direct inspiration on my dreams and aspirations."

Vivek told me a condensed version of the story of Brian Epstein and The Beatles.

Brian was a visionary, a gay man in Liverpool when being gay was a felony and Jewish at a time when anti–Semitism was pervasive. But he saw something in the relatively unknown Beatles, who were playing basement clubs and smoking and drinking onstage. Brian "cleaned them up," put them in suits, and gave them their signature haircuts. He then convinced Ed Sullivan to put them on his show, and he engineered Beatlemania. Vivek explained:

Brian was the ultimate outsider who had no cultural influence whatsoever. He chased his dreams. When he said The Beatles were going to be bigger than Elvis, they laughed at him. When he said The Beatles were going to elevate pop music into an art form, even he wasn't sure what that meant. He wasn't a big fan of pop music. He was a fan of music composers that will be remembered for all time, like Mozart and Beethoven. He saw that in John

68

and Paul. He thought that in hundreds of years, people would still be playing their compositions. Their songs are timeless.

Following his dream against all odds was something Vivek relates to personally. He grew up dreaming about a life in the arts but didn't know what that dream meant. He grew up to be a writer and producer as well as being known in the business as a sincerely good person who is kind to everyone. For me, there is no question about it. Brian's story helped me pursue my dreams.

Vivek's passion, talent, and perseverance paid off. His Broadway shows have won 25 Tony Awards from 44 nominations. But the research for *The Fifth Beatle* started long before any of that. Broadway was not the first path Vivek chose. He was a student at the Wharton School of Business when he decided to research Brian Epstein's life for his thesis. Vivek had no connections to anyone in The Beatles' world. He cold-contacted names he knew from books. "Everyone agreed to be interviewed," he said, still sounding surprised. He flew to Liverpool and conducted the interviews in person. "I was so interested in Brian's story that I forgot to be nervous."

Vivek's thesis turned into the *New York Times* best-selling graphic novel *The Fifth Beatle*. Soon after, NBC contacted him to develop it into a television series. To do a show about The Beatles' manager, he had to have the rights to The Beatles' music. He plunged ahead and contacted The Beatles' company, comprising Paul, Ringo, Olivia Harrison, and Yoko Ono. After three years of negotiations, they agreed to give the show full rights to the entire Beatles catalog. Recently, the show has been picked up by Disney Plus.

Vivek cannot definitively say way why the four agreed. "They didn't give me an answer other than yes," he said joyfully. But he has his own thoughts on why they did it. "I suspect it's because I was telling the Brian Epstein story and not retelling The Beatles story," he said. Vivek continued:

> They care a lot about Brian, especially as they get older. I'm telling a story that hasn't been told before. His management style was to hide the business from them. So, they didn't realize how much a manager does for the band. They made it clear that Brian deserves his due. They saw my heart was in the right place. I want to tell the story in a respectful, warts-and-all kind of way. I don't shy away from Brian being heroic; I wear that on my sleeve. But it's an honest portrayal of Brian. He's my historical mentor. He died in 1967, and I was born in 1973. His is someone's life I look to learn from. I learned not just what to do but also what not to do. Mentors have their failings. They are to learn and be inspired from.

An added benefit of the negotiations with the company was that Vivek met and got to know Paul, Ringo, Yoko, and Olivia. But that's not the first time he had contact with the two surviving Beatles. Vivek comes from a background of working in the music industry. "When I worked for Mercury Records, I worked on Ringo Starr's album *Vertical Man*, so that's the first time I met him," he said. "He was everything you'd want him to be. He was funny, grateful, warm, and engaging. Paul sent me a note—it was an email—about how much he loved *The Fifth Beatle*. He was complimenting me and our work! I thought it was one of my friends punking me. Paul liked something I did! It was incredibly surreal and amazing."

If you have not guessed by now, above all else, Vivek is a Beatles superfan, just like the rest of us.

"I'm a fan first," Vivek happily admitted. "You know that in the first 10 minutes. The business side wouldn't be happening without that. I've been researching Brian since college—1991. It took three and a half years to secure The Beatles' music rights; two and a half convincing Paul, Ringo, Olivia, and Yoko; and six months in negotiating the deal. Most producers wouldn't spend that kind of time. But time disappears when it's a labor of love. It fuels the business part of it."

The current plan for the show is six to eight episodes at one hour each. The book is a very slim 120 pages. Vivek said that the graphic novel is purposely short so people can read it in one sitting. "I was picturing an airport bookstore where someone who might not be a Beatles fan would see the drop-dead gorgeous artwork that Andrew Robinson and Kyle Baker did and a story that sounds interesting. It's something that you could easily finish by the time your flight lands. I wanted it to be easy to consume." The miniseries just makes the entire project even more exciting.

Vivek said that one of the hardest things to do when writing the book was to decide what to put in and what to leave out. One reason the miniseries is a joy for Vivek is that he gets to "put in so much stuff":

The people are very important. The book didn't include Pete Best, the first drummer before Ringo. If you're telling the story of The Beatles, it is irresponsible to leave out Pete Best. In the Brian Epstein story, it's not so irresponsible. In the eight-hour miniseries we do the Pete Best story, which is good because to this day I'm not sure if I made the right decision [in leaving him out.] The miniseries also gets into Brian's family much more deeply:

70

his mother, brother, and father. We see how Brian's mother was understanding about his sexual orientation and was something of a best friend. For his time and era, his father was incredibly supportive. It was difficult for him to understand his son's sexual orientation. He didn't totally get it the way his mother did, but he didn't think he was a freak.

But why in the 21st century is a book about The Beatles' manager so incredibly popular? "The Beatles still have a massive fan base," Vivek said. "People are always surprised when a new Beatles thing comes out and it sells better than people think it would." Vivek continued:

"But *The Fifth Beatle* at its heart is an inspirational human story. It's about a gay Jewish man at a time when being gay was a felony and anti–Semitism was pervasive. So, it is popular not only with Beatles fans but with the LGBTQ and the Jewish communities, [who both] supported the book. And the fourth element is that it's a comic. It's my first graphic novel. Kyle Baker and Andrew Robinson are well-respected artists. The book paints a picture of an important story. So, people say, 'Oh, the LGBTQ community supports this Beatles story; what's that all about?' or 'The Jewish community supports this comic book; what's that all about?' The bottom line is it's a human story. It belongs to all of us."

"In a way, this book has exposed members of the younger generation to Beatles music in a way that Rock Band [the video game based on Beatles music] exposed the gaming community to the music. I know for a fact that it has turned a ton of Beatle fans into comic fans."

And in the end, it's all about the message. "As corny as it sounds, The Beatles' message is all about love," Vivek added. "All You Need Is Love," "She Loves You." Brian had to literally hide his love away. That's why he enjoyed working with The Beatles. It was through them he was able to spread some love into the world. That's also why Beatles fans are a community rallied around a common theme with love at its core. The fans gravitate toward caring about each other. If you go to Beatles events, you see the same faces, and you are quick to become friends, or more than friends. I don't mean that in a sexual way. But I know that if I'm at a Beatles event and I get a call from home and I had to rush back, somebody would drive me to the airport; someone would get my bags from my room; someone would tell the facilitator that Vivek has to skip his panel. Beatles fans are a community and family.

"The band and their message are all about love, belonging, and inclusion. That message will always be needed. Whether it is 2018, 2088, or 1968, that message is always relevant. There will always be someone who feels like an outsider. Or feel something simple, like 'My parents don't understand me.' That's why The Beatles and their music will always have an appeal."

It All Started in Liverpool

Cavern City Tours director.

It could not be real. Here I was in Liverpool at the Cavern Club, waiting for the man who ran the show. I had an appointment for an interview, and I was a little nervous. The cashier at the ticket booth called the office. The director sent an assistant to come get me and escort me to the main office around the corner. His assistant could have been a Beatle himself. He had the haircut and the adorable Liverpudlian accent, and he wasn't hard on the eyes. When he said "Follow me," in my imagination I said *I'll follow you anywhere.*

The adorable assistant brought me into the Cavern City Tours office, and I hit the jackpot. It was filled with young men who looked and sounded just like him. I thought I had died and gone to heaven. Then he introduced me to the head honcho, Bill Heckle, co-owner of Cavern City Tours, the umbrella company that runs the Cavern Club and the Magical Mystery Tour, the sightseeing tour around Liverpool. The tour bus itself is a replica of the one in the film. Bill was warm and welcoming, and he had a great sense of humor and an equally great Liverpudlian accent. As he led me into the conference room, he put me at ease when he pointed to the name on the door: "Boredroom." Listening to his story, boredom was the last thing that came to mind.

After we were seated, I took out my notebook and turned my voice recorder on. I looked down at my notebook. The first thing Bill said was "The Beatles are more popular than Shakespeare!"

I knew I had to look up. I was not going to miss a minute of this story by taking notes. I let the recorder do its job.

"I guarantee, now, in this period—I bet my life on this knowledge—if you pick a hundred places around the world, remote as you want, and you ask people, 'Recite me a line from Shakespeare or sing me a line from a Beatles song,' I know damn well that The Beatles will annihilate Shakespeare!"

That sums up Bill Heckle's feelings about the band and promoting Beatles tourism in Liverpool. As one of the directors of Cavern City

72

Tours, he runs the rebuilt Cavern Club, where The Beatles played 292 times since their start there in February 1961. The club is still a hot nightspot in Liverpool, where bands and singers including The Who, Adele, and Jessie J have played. But the biggest draw for Beatles fans are the Cavern Club Beatles. The tribute band is one of the best in the world, embodying not only the voices and the music but also every unique movement of John, Paul, George, and Ringo. The setting can't be beat. Every inch of the walls is covered in photos and sculptures of The Beatles' days there.

After enjoying a night filled with the fantasy of seeing The Beatles live, you can board the Magical Mystery Tour bus, which Bill himself ran more than 100 times. It now takes 70,000 people a year to old Beatles haunts throughout Liverpool, including the church where John and Paul met for the first time, and then on to Penny Lane and Strawberry Field.

When John Lennon was growing up, Strawberry Field was an orphanage run by the Salvation Army, and he could see it over his backyard fence. The story goes that John would hang in the tree above the field to watch the girls. His aunt Mimi, who raised him, would tell John he would get hung up there, thus the line "Nothing to get hung about." The bus takes you by all four childhood homes and stops for photo ops, then goes on to lots of other historical Beatles spots.

As if that's not enough, Cavern City Tours also runs the megapopular International Beatleweek. Held annually during the last week in August, it features 70 tribute bands from 20 countries. Fans from all over the world pack the hotels, streets, and performance venues. Since its inception more than 40 years ago, 900 bands have played from 47 countries. There are 500 gigs in the week at 12 venues, with 60 bands playing on any given day. "The Beatles family is immense," Bill said. "It goes all over the world."

International Beatleweek brings people back time and time again. Fans from different countries will meet and become lifelong friends, vowing to see each other the same time next year. Some even travel to each other's homes. And some, whom you'll see in chapter 4, fall in love and get married. "That's what happens when you bring people with common interests into an environment like this," Bill said. The company's 30 employees are all Beatles lovers. "It would be impossible to run a business such as this without a real love for the band and their music," Bill said.

Bill is a first-generation fan who encountered Beatles music for the first time in August 1962, when he was just six years old. The story picks up with Bill visiting his grandmother's house:

"I had never seen my grandmother shout. But she was going ape at Aunty Joyce, who was 16. Grandmother had eight kids; Aunty Joyce was the second youngest. They lived in a small house, two bedrooms upstairs and two rooms downstairs. They were working class. My father told me later what happened. Aunty Joyce at 16 just lost her first job. The money she brought home was important to the family. Well, it turned out the reason was Aunty Joyce worked on Victoria Street [a few blocks from the Cavern Club]. At lunch she would go see The Beatles. She would be late getting back to work. She got warning after warning. Finally, she got sacked."

"The following week, we went to my maternal grandmother's. Same thing was happening over there. Grandmother was yelling at Aunty Francis, who was also 16. Aunty Francis was in grammar school, which goes from age 11 to 18. You have to take a test at age 11 to get into grammar school, which leads to university. You have to be smart to get into grammar school. After you're in, you take an exam every year, and the results are released in August. Grandmother woke up Aunty Francis to tell her to go in today to get the results. Aunty Francis said she wasn't feeling well. So, my grandmother went to the school to get the results herself."

The headmistress met Bill's grandmother at the school and said, "How's Francis? We were so worried." Bill's grandmother was confused and assured the headmistress that Francis was fine. She'd only been sick for a couple of days. Then she got the shock of her life. "No, she hasn't been in for four months because she's in the hospital," the headmistress said, her face creased with concern. "She hasn't taken any exams. I have all the documentation for four months."

Apparently, Aunty Francis would "make like she was calling on her friend around the corner to walk to school together," Bill said. "Both sets of parents went to work at 7:30. As soon as her parents left, they would change out of their uniforms, put their lipstick on, and—you know damn well where this is going—they would go to the Cavern to see The Beatles. This was happening for four months!"

Something special was obviously happening in Liverpool in August before the October release of The Beatles' first single. At that time, the city was in decline. Once the largest port in the world, Liverpool was dark, dank, and depressed and still had bombed-out sites.

"You read about what happened in 1963, but I have direct proof,"

Bill said. "They [The Beatles] went and got a record deal. The first week of 1963, John moved to London. There was a big backlash in the city. It was almost like 1966, when people were burning Beatle albums. There was a backlash on The Beatles in Liverpool."

The Beatles backlash was great for Bill, who was only seven years old. His young aunties were now anti–Beatles and gave him their first four albums and singles. He was hooked. After that, for every birthday and Christmas he would get Beatles gifts. He didn't have to buy anything himself. Finally, at 13, he bought his first album: *Abbey Road.*

As an adult, Bill is a walking encyclopedia on the history of Beatles tourism in Liverpool.

After John's death, there was a huge outpouring of affection in Liverpool. That led to the first attempt at Beatles tourism. Bill started the first Magical Mystery Tours. Beatles City, a museum with great exhibits, opened its doors. But it didn't make it. Two short years later, Beatles City's doors closed for good.

The original Cavern Club was demolished in 1973 and became a parking lot because of a compulsory purchase order by the government. They needed to build a ventilation shaft for an underground train that never ran. The Cavern Club was later authentically reconstructed using 15,000 bricks from the original building. It opened its doors in 1984 and changed hands five times, failing every time. "People were in it for the wrong reasons," Bill said.

Bill was a teacher when he started Cavern City Tours in 1983. "I was a teacher, teaching history," Bill said. "Teaching Beatles history was a lot more fun." The company started with the Magical Mystery Tour bus that was so successful on its first run, then grew into running the Cavern Club very successfully. Tens of thousands of fans visit the Cavern Club and take the tour bus annually.

All these people ... where do they all come from? When the Cavern opened, its biggest fan base were American and Japanese tourists. But through the decades, there has been a massive change. Now Brazilian fans fill the Cavern in droves. The influx of Brazilians is the result of a latent Beatlemania in Brazil that started in 1990 when Paul McCartney took his tour there and played a lot of Beatles favorites. In fact, he was the first Beatle to ever play there. He played for two nights to 200,000 people a night. Beatles music is now so popular in Brazil that a new Cavern Club replica was built there.

"The average age of a Beatles fan in Brazil is 28," Bill said. "The average age here is about 60. At the Cavern we see people 8 to 80, but people who go to see Paul in concert are largely an older audience. In Brazil it's kids."

Kids all over the world, not just in Brazil, are finding Beatles music. Bill said that 14- and 15-year-olds are finding it on iTunes and Spotify. Beatles music is organically accessible, not something you have to hear over and over again to appreciate. Once kids are hooked, they become secretive, even protective, about it and share it with their friends. That's how Beatles music is spreading among younger people, not from parents to kids.

Sixty years out, the market for The Beatles is still growing. "It's growing in terms of history," Bill said. John's death was the horrible catalyst that put The Beatles into history, but nothing can "devalue the music" or "interfere with the amazing body of work they've done." The passing of George cemented the historical place of the Beatles further. "Sadly, when the final Beatle goes, they will be consigned to their history," Bill said. "In 1983 I said on television that The Beatles will be recognized as bigger than Shakespeare. I was ridiculed by a politician. But I bet my life it's true."

After we were finished with our chat, Bill was kind enough to give me two tickets to the Cavern Club to see the Cavern Club Beatles that night. I took my traveling companion, my 19-year-old daughter. That night, we walked down the long flight of steps that led to the Cavern Club front stage. It looked just as it did in all of the pictures in all of the Beatles books I have read all my life. I imagined I was one of Bill's teenage aunties walking down the dank, dark staircase, skipping school and work, in my miniskirt, high heels, and bright lipstick back when it was all beginning ... if only. In my mind's ear, I could hear the music swelling from the stage as the young Beatles sweat their brains out playing the raucous tunes of Little Richard, Carl Perkins, and the rest. I could hear Paul belting out the words to "Long Tall Sally." In my imagination, when I made it down the steps, I could feel the sweat coming off the stage and pouring off the walls as Paul shook his head madly. I was dancing like crazy like everyone else in the club. I made eye contact with George, and he winked.

In real life, I could smell the beer and sweat of the crowd. I fought to get up close, as the aunties would have. The real Cavern was crowded but not with teenagers of days gone by. The walls were covered in photos of The Beatles giving it their all for the crowd. Then I noticed a closed curtain between the front room and the lounge, giving an aura of exclusivity. The bouncers at the curtain asked for 10 pounds each. I handed them my handwritten card from Bill himself, and ta-da, they drew the curtain back. We felt like royalty.

My heart went boom when I crossed that room. Was it them? The Cavern Club Beatles looked and sounded so much like the real thing, and the setting completed the dream. They had the crowd in the palms of their hands. Not only did they have the band down musically, but the lads on the stage were also tall and lanky just like the Fab Four, each member almost a double for the Beatle he was representing.

Everyone was on their feet dancing and singing along gleefully. Even my daughter was getting into it. At 19, she called herself "a fan by association." She's been hearing the music all her life. She was right there singing along.

That's the magic of The Beatles! And the band played on ...

The Teachers That Teach Me Are Cool

The Liverpool Institute of Performing Arts,
cofounded by Paul McCartney and Mark Featherstone-Witty.

Imagine you are an emerging singer-songwriter. Now imagine your mentor is Paul McCartney. Students at the Liverpool Institute of

Paul McCartney and Mark Featherstone-Witty, cocreators of the Liverpool Institute for Performing Arts, on July 25, 2019.

Exterior of the Liverpool Institute for Performing Arts, August 1994.

Performing Arts (LIPA) don't have to imagine. It's all real. Paul mentors the songwriting class. As a matter of fact, every graduating LIPA student gets to shake Paul's hand after he hands them their diplomas! There are fewer than 1,000 students at the school, and I'm bettting right about now you wish you were one of them.

So why does Paul do these things, and why at this school? Paul played a large part in creating the school with British entrepreneur Mark Featherstone-Witty. Now it's Paul's baby. He hosts meets and greets where the proceeds go to the school. A portion of his sound check proceeds go to the school, and he always gives a good quote or two when the school needs some publicity.

Mark Featherstone-Witty kindly took time out of his busy schedule to tell me about the origins and the success of the school that started as a dream. It all began with two completely unrelated events in the mid–80s. Paul was writing to the *Liverpool Oratorio* about a young boy growing up in Liverpool. There's quite a big section about a boy going to school. Paul decided to revisit his old school, the Liverpool Institute High School for Boys, which he and George both attended. Paul took a cameraman around in the dead of the night, and you can see these scenes in the box set *Echos*. Paul reminisces about his time in school. It's a wonderful picture of the school as it then was—derelict.

The high school was left empty when the population in the area declined. Paul told Beatles producer George Martin that he wanted to restore the building. George knew that Mark was interested in developing a performing arts school. Mark had already created the BRIT School for Performing Arts and Technology with Richard Branson, founder of the Virgin Group, and George Martin had been involved in that project. The BRIT School is supported by the British Record Industry Trust and is free for 14- to 19-year-old students. In the States it would be considered a high school.

Mark wanted to develop a college-level school. "George [Martin] told Paul that he was involved in developing this school in London with me and said, 'Why don't you two meet?' Paul wanted to rebuild the building, and I wanted to have another go at a performing arts school, not for people in their teens but older. That's how we got together and embarked on an adventure in which we had no idea and no experience."

Paul and Mark got the school off the ground, but Paul was not sold on the idea of performing arts being taught in a college setting. "Paul regarded himself as self-taught. He didn't associate learning with being

Paul McCartney, Mark Featherstone-Witty, and a LIPA graduating student in July 2012. All graduates get to shake Paul's hand on graduation day.

in a building or school or college. The fact is you can learn anytime, anywhere. He was very adept at learning from people around him.... It took him a while to appreciate my version."

Paul finally did gain that appreciation when he held a memorial service for his late wife, Linda, in London. By this time the school was already up and running, and students from LIPA performed at the event. Music legends such as Elton John and Sting told Paul he was doing a great job with those kids. That started to convince Paul that Mark was on the right track. "Now Paul says we're one of the best performing arts schools in the country."

Schools all over the world are now modeling their curricula after LIPA, but when it opened its doors in 1996, its program was unique. While creating the school, Mark asked various "survivors" of the music business what they would have liked to have known when they left school that they had to learn the hard way. Each had their own unique perspective.

George Martin said that everybody should appreciate what everyone else is doing to create an event. "That's the kernel of what we have here at LIPA," Mark said. "There is a very heavy emphasis on collaboration and negotiation."

Joan Armatrading told Mark that she didn't know what was going on when she signed her first contract. So, at LIPA everyone has to understand that even though performing is an art, it is also a business, and they must operate with business awareness. "This was an idea that was quite unique 25 years ago," Mark said.

For Mark, creating performing arts schools combines two of his lifelong dreams. "At 18, I put on a show with my school at the time. I thought my future would be in acting," he recalled. "But I also directed and produced." He realized it wasn't just performing that he enjoyed; what he really loved was the thrill of putting something together from scratch. "I started four or five businesses by myself and with other people," he said. "When I would start my own business, there was risk, and risk means excitement."

After starting different businesses, Mark realized that the show was what he enjoyed the most. The idea of a performing arts high school struck when he saw the film *Fame*, about a fictional performing arts school in New York. That was the start of BRIT, then on to LIPA. Currently, LIPA boasts the largest enrollment of non–British students at the undergraduate level of any school in the United Kingdom, with students from 41 different countries.

"The fact that Paul's name is attached has an enormous influence," Mark said. "This school simply would not exist without Paul McCartney."

In His Life

The John Lennon story on the Broadway stage.

Look for the story of John Lennon's early life in Liverpool and the formation of The Beatles on Broadway in the near future. The show was inspired by the brilliant biopic aptly titled *Nowhere Boy*, which in turn was inspired by the jaw-dropping book written by John's half sister, Julia Baird.

Julia shared the same mother with the legend and is in fact her namesake. The book depicts John's struggle to please his mother and his aunt Mimi, who had legal custody of him. Strict, rule-following Mimi was the polar opposite of fun-loving musician Julia. The theatrical production will delve even deeper into the conflict between the two sisters, both of whom had a profound influence over John Lennon's life.

I met with lead producer Robyn Goodman, founder and CEO of Aged in Wood Productions (*Avenue Q, In the Heights, Rodgers & Hammerstein's Cinderella*) and her coproducing team, Dayna and Brian Lee, founders of AF Creative Media (*Moulin Rouge, Company*). They were warm, inviting, and clearly passionate about the story and its significance. What's more, all of them have won Tony Awards.

"Think of it as a play with music, not a musical," Robyn pointed out. "We don't want to see John singing about how he wants to be a star." The show will be filled with the music that inspired The Beatles, including Carl Perkins, Roy Orbison, and Elvis. John and Paul's pre–Beatles band, the Quarrymen, covered their songs, as did The Beatles in early days. The play will include Beatles music as well, but "we'll present the music in such a way that even for fanatics, it will be like hearing it for the first time," Robyn promised.

Those same fanatics may also be familiar with the story of John's formative years but have never seen it in this dynamic new form. The details will all be there. John was born to Julia and Alfred Lennon on October 9, 1940. Alfred, a merchant marine, abandoned the family, went off to sea, and never sent a penny in child support, much less a letter to let Julia know his whereabouts. A few years after his disappearance, Julia met Bobby Baird. Unable to legally divorce Alfred, she moved

81

in with Bobby. Julia's sister, Mimi, John's aunt, had Julia legally declared an unfit mother because of her living situation. Mimi was awarded custody of John and proceeded to raise him, according to Julia Baird's book.

As a teenager, John discovered that his mother lived within walking distance of Mendips, the home where he grew up. Despite the proximity, Mimi would not allow John to see her. John, always a rebel, snuck out, cut school, and did whatever was necessary to get to know his free-spirited mother. At this point, Julia and Bobby had two daughters, Julia and Jackie. Julia's family loved John, and to the girls he was a goofy big brother. His mother taught him how to play the banjo and shared her love of music with him. John relentlessly traveled in the shadows to spend time with his other family. Often Julia would try to visit John at Mendips, but she couldn't get past Mimi.

Eventually the two wore Mimi down, and she allowed Julia into her home. It seemed as if the sisters had called a truce, and John was finally able to see his mom in the light of day. John was 17 when Julia was visiting at Mendips. She left the house to walk home with plans to see John soon after. Tragically, she stepped off the curb and got hit by a car. She died instantly. The shock reverberated through John's soul. Her sudden death resulted in cementing his relationship with Paul McCartney, who at age 15 had already lost his mother to cancer. At the time of Julia's death, the duo was already a songwriting team and performing as the Quarrymen.

The play will focus on the two women who raised one of the greatest musicians in the world. "We are looking to peel back the curtain on the two women," Dayna said. "It's a story about two female leading ladies and how they influenced him. They both obviously impacted his life so much. You can see this by just looking at his later writing, his songs, and his catalog."

Robyn agreed, saying there were many layers to Mimi and Julia:

When you look at interviews with [the late] Mimi, you can see her underlying objective was to make sure we knew how much John loved her. He did love her. He called her every Sunday. But I think he loved his mother too. She was a bigger influence. His lack of her was a bigger influence. Mimi just gave him boundaries and order, so he felt safer with her than he might have with Julia. Mimi made [Julia] out to be psychotic and said she was [sleeping] around. It was the '40s. Morals were different. There was no legal recourse for Julia. She couldn't divorce.

This story is pre–Beatles and offers a fresh take on the band's history for many people. "For a lot of North American culture, The Beatles exist post–*Ed Sullivan*," Brian said. "This story is before that."

On a deeper look, it's also the story of what makes an artist, Robyn added. "What can we bring out about these two women that made John a real artist, not just a banjo player? A real force in music? That's going to be the tricky part to tease out, but it's there."

Mimi and Julia weren't the only influence in John's life. There were two male role models as well, his uncle George—Mimi's husband, who died when John was a teen—and Bobby Baird, Julia's live-in boyfriend. "There were suggestions [in the biopic] that John was close to Mimi's husband, that they had common ground. Whether it was music or drinking, we're not sure. We have to explore that," Robyn said.

"The interesting thing about [John] meeting Yoko is that he 'got therapy.' He was able to write *Mother*, which is like a primal cry that must have been buried in him his whole life, especially after losing her. I think people who lose a parent early on all have that primal scream. He tapped into it with Yoko."

In her book *John*, Cynthia, John's first wife, says that in some ways John felt safe with Yoko as he did with Mimi. Yoko "provided boundaries," Robyn said, "but she also released something in him."

I asked the producers why they think this show will be important in the 2020s, 40 years after John's death and 50 years after The Beatles split up. "You're going to see a part of yourself in it," Dayna said, "wanting to grow outside your circumstances, finding yourself in adolescence. It's tough growing up, and that has not changed for anybody," she added emphatically.

For a lot of people, this will also be an eye-opening biography about the young John Lennon. "Some people don't know how his mother died," Robyn said. "It'll deepen their compassion and understanding. It did for me. Later in life, you read all kinds of things about him. Who knows what was true and what wasn't? But to find out that this woman took him away from his mother and that he snuck out as a teenager to get to know her and learn music from her, and then she was hit by a car … just that alone."

In and of itself, the show is an artist's story. "There was escapism in his music," Brian said, "the ability for this young man to have his music to express himself, which so many people don't have. Then he happens to become the greatest musician of all time. It's fascinating."

The show is also a look into what The Beatles' songs may actually be about. "When you hear so many of The Beatles' songs, you think they are about a love interest or a woman," Dayna said. "But you hear the stories of Paul and John's mothers, and you realize these songs could be about their mothers."

Ultimately, the show is about the universal story of the connection between mother and child. "I had a friend who just lost her mother," Robyn said thoughtfully. "Her relationship with her mother was complicated, like all of ours. But when I said 'Hello,' she started sobbing. The connection and longing for a mother never stop, even if she lives until her child is 76. Someone is always someone's child."

As you might expect, all of the show's producers are big Beatles fans. Robyn is a first-generation fan who remembers watching *The Ed Sullivan Show* on February 9, 1964. "I didn't understand all those girls screaming," Robyn recalled, "but I sang 'I Want to Hold Your Hand' every day for the next year."

It's different for Dayna and Brian, who were both born in 1989. Dayna learned to love the music from her father, who is still a huge fan. In Dayna's childhood home, half the basement was dedicated to her father's Beatles memorabilia collection. Her love was solidified by her mother. "It was always playing in the car whether I was with my mom or my dad," she said. "And now the generation below us is exposed to the music in commercials. Even if you're not a fan, you know the music. Familiarity is so special."

Brian's parents were more into Herman's Hermits, he said. But Brian and Dayna met at the Berklee College of Music, where there's a class on the music of John Lennon. There are music theory classes where they analyze the music of The Beatles, and they use Beatles music in orchestration class. The "most prestigious music school in the world is using The Beatles' scores to teach us music theory and how to write a song," Brian said emphatically.

Then there was the shocking end of John's life, when he was murdered at gunpoint. What are these three storytellers' memories of that moment in time?

"I was having dinner with friends on the West Side not too far away," Robyn said. "We were in shock. We couldn't believe someone would do that in front of his wife. What kind of person would do that in front of his home? All of my friends were devastated. We talked for hours and hours. As a generation we had Kennedy. I was very young; Kennedy was horrible, and our parents were devastated, but this was bigger for us. John was ours."

Dayna and Brian were born after John's murder, yet they still felt it. "My father told me that was one of the only days in his life when he cried," Dayna said. "John was such an advocate for social justice and art. It makes you wonder what he would be advocating for today."

For these reasons and many more, this new show depicting John's early years will resonate with people of every generation. "It's always important," Robyn said. "It's The Beatles."

The Magical History Tour

Step right this way. Roll up for the Magical History Tour run by Charles F. Rosenay!!! [the exclamation points are part of his name] of Liverpool Tours, based in Connecticut.

If you're a Beatles fan, you've got to get this tour into your life. "You get to walk the walk of The Beatles," said Batya Selevan, who's been a tour guest more than 20 times.

The trip leaves from New York and heads to London, where you go to all the major Beatles sites, and then continues on to International Beatleweek in Liverpool for seven days, where the party never stops. "It's not a senior citizen tour where you take in the sights, have dinner at 5:00, and go to bed," Charles said. "After dinner, the night is young. We go to concerts and dance all night long. You're with kindred spirits enjoying everything Beatles."

Yes, there are other ways to see the sights, but when you are with the Magical History Tour, you get access to things you couldn't get on your own. Batya has had the opportunity to make a recording at Abbey Road Studios in the same room where The Beatles recorded. Not too many people can say that. She has also met Beatle family members and other notables associated with the lads, including Paul's brother, Mike; John's half sister, Julia; and a classmate of John's who took the group on a tour of their old haunts as kids. They met The Beatles original drummer Pete Best and his mom, Mona Best, as well as the sister of the original Beatles' bass player, Stuart Sutcliffe.

"On this trip, you never know who you're going to meet or see," Batya said. "Beatles people come to the Liverpool convention [held at a popular hotel during Beatleweek] and just walk around like everybody else. You can shake hands with them, and you don't have to pay for their autograph."

There's something new to discover on every trip, Batya said.

A party DJ/actor/author and entertainer by trade, Charles has dedicated his life to The Beatles. He started Liverpool Productions when he was a teenager in 1978. That same year, he started The Beatles Expo: The New York/New England Beatles Convention, which took place for many years in Connecticut. He has promoted conventions and festivals in many cities in the United States and overseas. Charles published and wrote *Good Day Sunshine*, a Beatles fanzine from 1981 until the mid–'90s, when the internet made it obsolete. It was also in the early '80s when he started running the Magical History Tours taking American fans to England.

Charles's first memory in life is standing in front of the television watching *The Ed Sullivan Show* on February 9, 1964. He was completely mesmerized. "Every guy wanted to be a Beatle. Every girl wanted to marry one," he said. Charles did not have any musical talent, so he did the next best thing and became a collector. His parents bought him all of the 45s, and instead of pinning the jackets to his walls as most kids did, he saved everything in pristine condition. Inspired by the Beatles-fest in New York run by Mark Lapidos and the Boston conventions run by Joe Pope, Charles sold part of his collection to finance his first expo while he was still in high school. It was held at the New Haven Motor Inn with six vendors and a local New Haven tribute band.

The expos grew after Charles started taking tour groups to Liverpool in the early '80s. In those days, Liverpool wasn't the thriving Beatles tourism mecca that it is today. "The first time I went to Liverpool in 1983, the Cavern wasn't rebuilt yet," Charles said. The Cavern Club is where The Beatles played 292 times before they came to America. "To visit the Cavern, you had to put your head against the ground and imagine. The city was dingy and gray. The best thing about Liverpool were the people and the fact that The Beatles came from there," Charles recalled. At that time he would bring 60 American tourists, and Beatles insiders would clamor to tell them their stories. Early on, Charles became friends with Cynthia, John's first wife; Allan Williams, The Beatles' first manager; Pete Best, the drummer before Ringo; Beatles promoter Sam Leach; Cavern DJ Bob Wooler; Apple manager Alistar Taylor; Beatles chauffeur Alf Bicknell; The Beatles' tailor Gordon Millings; and others who were all a part of Beatles history. Charles brought these people who were there when it happened back to the United States as guests at his conventions. For some of them, it was their first appearance at an American convention. Word got around, and the expo became a well-known destination.

Charles also interviewed many of these Beatles insiders for his magazine *Good Day Sunshine*, which was one of the three largest Beatles fan magazines of its time. "Everyone involved in Beatles history was very easy to talk to at that time," he said. He garnered interviews with

86

Ringo's stepdad; Paul's brother, Mike; and many other family members of the band.

In 1984 the Cavern Club was rebuilt across the street from the original location, using 15,000 authentic bricks from the demolished site. Much to his delight, Charles is now a Liverpool insider working side by side with his sister company, Cavern City Tours, Liverpool's largest tour operator. Cavern City Tours runs the rebuilt Cavern Club, International Beatleweek, and the Magical Mystery Tour bus, a two-hour guided tour of Beatles sites around Liverpool.

Charles generously shared his connections with me, and many of them are spotlighted in this book. He introduced me to the director of Cavern City Tours, Bill Heckle, who in turn introduced me to couples who met and got married at Beatleweek, international tribute bands, and more. Beatles people are sincerely a worldwide family, and Charles said that he feels privileged to be a part of them. "My career has paid off in ways beyond money," he said. He's lucky enough to have met three of The Beatles. Paul and Ringo know his name! Sadly, he never got to meet John.

Charles's place in Beatles history was cemented when Ringo placed a portion of his personal collection on auction for charity, and *Good Day Sunshine* magazine was among the items. "Right there with sets of drumsticks and his personal clothing was a collection of my magazine. It's one of my proudest moments," Charles said.

"I'm blessed that what I do brings people so much joy as it does myself."

For more information on the Magical Mystery Tours, please visit Liverpooltours.com.

Four

Love Is All You Need

The Beatles' message was all about peace and love. It is no surprise that Beatle lovers come together as family. Tight friendships across the globe are born at Beatles festivals, conventions, and Beatles fans' mecca, Liverpool—especially Liverpool during International Beatleweek.

For some fans, love is truly all you need. These couples found each other, fell in love, and got married because of their dedication to John, Paul, George, and Ringo.

Let's All Get Up and Dance to a Song

"Your mother should know" could be the soundtrack to Hope and Laurence Juber's (LJ former lead guitarist in Wings) love story. The uncanny journey that led up to their serendipitous meeting all started when Hope's worried mother told her to get her hair done. The beauty salon in Beverly Hills led to a chance meeting with Ringo, which led to her working on the Paramount lot in Hollywood, which led to her dating Robin Williams, which led her to a trip to New York, which ultimately landed her in the right place at the right time to meet the former lead guitarist for Wings, Laurence "LJ" Juber, and live happily ever after.

Here's the story of a lovely marriage. Hope Juber nee Schwartz is the daughter of famous television producer Sherwood Schwartz. You may not know his name, but you know his number. Sherwood Schwartz created the shows that shaped a generation, *The Brady Bunch* and *Gilligan's Island*. To Hope he was just dear old Dad.

Hope's Beatles story begins like most of her generation in America. The 1964 *Ed Sullivan Show*. She fell instantly in love at seven years old.

"Growing up people knew two things about me," Hope said. "They knew that I had red hair and they knew I loved The Beatles."

George Harrison, Hope Juber, Laurence Juber, and baby Ilsey the day George gave two-day-old Ilsey the gift of music in April 1986.

Their music soothed, cheered, and inspired Hope all through the arc of their career, which coincided with her formative years. She grew up to follow in her dad's footsteps and become a writer. In college she wrote a play that consisted entirely of Beatles lyrics all the while collecting memorabilia.

"I was never the screaming-on-the-other-side-of-the-fence Beatle fan, but their music just meant everything to me."

Cut to graduating college, writing, and working to sell scripts when the shot rang out that was heard around the world.

John Lennon's murder shattered Hope. She went into a massive depression during which she couldn't eat or get out of bed.

"It was like the world went dark."

Therapy didn't help. Hope's worried parents were at their wit's end. Her mother, at the end of her rope, told Hope to get her hair done to make herself feel better.

"It was ludicrous! I was having an existential breakdown, and she wanted me to get my hair done. But she was Mom, and I knew she was worried, so I said okay."

While Hope was sitting in the salon chair, the stylist was fussing with her hair and couldn't help noticing how sad she was. She told him why, and he told her to take a walk around the block while he finished with his last client and then they would talk over coffee.

Dejected, she walked the streets of Beverly Hills with her head down.

"I was going along, not looking where I was going, and I ended up— BAM—I walked right into somebody. I'm standing on a pair of boots—I look up and I'm standing on Ringo Starr. In the middle of Beverly Hills, I was on his feet! He was there with Barbara. And I was like, 'I'm so sorry that I stepped on you. I apologize.' And then I said, 'I'm just so sorry about John.' I turned to leave, and he said, 'Hold on a minute. Can I talk to you for a minute?' I said, 'Sure,' and I turned."

Ringo told her about his relationship with John. He told her he was working on a new album and that was a focus for him because work was really something that could pull you through. For him, working on this new album was helping him through his loss of John.

"He gave me this kind of amazing philosophy and pep talk just in the middle of Beverly Hills. I did not know him from anybody, but clearly it was easy to read me, and it was clear that I was having a hard time with this, and he was just really generous with his time."

Ringo's words reverberated in the back of Hope's mind when her dad called and asked her to work on a new show with him. She usually turned her father down, wanting to make a name for herself on her own, but she remembered Ringo saying work that could help pull you through, and she realized this was her opportunity. She said yes.

Hope went to work as a writer on *The Brady Brides*, on the Paramount lot. She quickly moved up to story editor working on all the scripts. Their soundstage was next door to the *Mork & Mindy* soundstage.

"I was always a fan of comedy, and a fan of the show, and a fan of Robin Williams. I ended up running into him all the time at Paramount, and we ended up in a relationship."

Robin was headed to New York to shoot *The World According to Garp*. As soon as Hope had a break from her shooting schedule, she hopped on a plane to New York to visit. One day Robin had to do an interview and told her he would meet her later at the famous comedy club Catch a Rising Star.

If this were a movie, the music would be coming to a crescendo, because this was the final scene before Hope's world shifted on its axis.

The serendipitous meeting was foreshadowed as soon as Hope walked into the club.

Four. Love Is All You Need

"I heard a couple of people talking, and one of them said to the other that Paul McCartney's guitar player was there that night. I didn't really know the members of Wings, but I kind of registered that and thought 'That's cool.'"

Hope sat at the bar and was talking to a woman named Cathy, who turned out to be a singer and asked if she wanted to meet the musicians she was working with.

"These three men started walking toward us, and Laurence was in the middle. It was one of those movie moments where everything else kind of went wavy and blurry and faded away and it was just him and me. Everything shifted. I ended up forgetting all about why I was in New York in the first place, forgot about Robin, and I ended up going out for dinner that evening with Laurence. And we left, we're having dinner, and he invited me back to his apartment there in New York. I walked in the door, and I saw this big Wings poster. And I saw him *in* the Wings poster. It hadn't occurred to me until that moment that that's who they were talking about. And I said, 'Wait a minute, that's you!' And he said, 'Yeah, I was in that band.'"

The conversation led to the fact that Laurence was working on an album with Paul and Ringo called *Stop and Smell the Roses*. That was the album Ringo was talking about that day in Beverly Hills. Hope decided to stay in New York another week, and the rest is history.

"That's how I met Laurence. You can see how it went from John's death to Ringo to Paul. I mean, I don't know how much more Beatle-related it can get."

Their love story is just the beginning of this tale. Do you want to hear about the time George Harrison blessed famoussinger-songwriter Ilsey Juber—yes, the Jubers' daughter—with the gift of music?

For Hope there was that one Beatle that was missing, and she knew she had to correct that. After all, George was always her Beatle. When she was pregnant with their second daughter, Laurence was working with George on *Shanghai Surprise*.

"I really wanted to meet George. I had always been a guitar fan, and George was my Beatle and I was very excited about the possibility of going to the studio to meet George."

Laurence made arrangements for the very pregnant Hope to join them in the studio the next day, and she would get a chance to spend some time talking to George.

"I was so happy about that, and then that evening I went into labor! I was like, 'No! I can't have this baby now! I'm going into the studio tomorrow to meet George. I can't possibly have this baby!'" Instead of "Here Comes the Sun" it was "Here Comes the Daughter." Hope gave birth to Ilsey, and the next morning Laurence went off to the studio to work with George.

"I'm in the hospital with Ilsey, and the phone rings and it's George Harrison! He said, 'I hear you just had a baby. I would love to meet you, and I would love to meet the baby as soon you're able to just bring her down to the studio.'"

The first place Ilsey ever went was a recording studio. She was just two days old. The studio was a big cavernous room with wood floors.

"George came and lifted her out of the baby carrier; he went into the studio and started dancing. He's holding her, and he's just dancing around the floor. It was very magical, so we all kind of stood back and let him have this moment. He was talking to her in a different language— Sanskrit—and he was just holding her. He did this for quite awhile. And after, I guess he felt like he needed to give her back to me. He walked over and he was handing her to me, and I said, 'What did you say to her?' Because at the very end of him dancing he took his finger, and he touched the middle of her forehead and said something in Sanskrit and handed her to me. I said, 'What was that you said to her?' And he said, 'Well, I was feeling the energy of this new life, and I just had the feeling that I really wanted to give her the gift of music, so I did."

Ilsey is a hit songwriter now. But the way she came to learn music indeed was magical. She started out as a drummer. She took up drums when she was about 11 years old, and by the time she was 13 she was playing drums in a jazz band with adults in clubs. Hope and Laurence were convinced they had a drummer.

"One day she picked up the guitar, and she was terrible. She was like plunk, plunk and that was it. We thought, 'well that's okay she doesn't have to play guitar—she's a drummer.' The next week she walks into the room—picks up Laurence's guitar—and starts playing blues leads. We said, 'When did you learn how to do that?' And she said, I mean literally she was almost frozen, and she said, 'I don't know. I don't know how I'm doing it. I can't stop my fingers.' Boom, she could play guitar. Two weeks later she could play keyboards. And then she started writing these songs. And we just went 'Thank you, George.'"

Ilsey is now in her mid–30s and has "The gift of music" in Sanskrit tattooed on her wrist.

Hope feels a very strong pull and connection to The Beatles. The family good-heartedly calls themselves "Beatles adjacent."

"I had the opportunity to meet three out of the four and have it be in a situation where there were personal moments with each one that I feel very thankful that that has happened, and I never would have imagined that I would be in a situation like that growing up."

Hope has produced Laurence's acoustic music of The Beatles and Wings albums. The two have worked together on many projects including soundtracks to movies she has been a part of. The pair honestly feel they are soulmates.

Hope reflects on the fact the John Lennon's murder was the catalyst that brought her to meet the love of her life. But she feels certain it didn't have to be that way. Fate would have brought the two together another way.

" I often think about the fact that had I the choice of meeting Laurence the way I did, because it really all started from when John got killed. To be able to change that I would. I would change that."

A Day in the Life

August 8, 2019, was a big day in Beatles history. It marked the 50th anniversary of the famous photo shoot for one of the most famous album covers of all time, *Abbey Road*. A star-studded party was held inside the studio, where Paul and Ringo were honored guests. Outside, the streets were jammed with Beatles fans from all over the world. Reporters and photographers clamored for the story. The crowd was so big that buses couldn't get by, and traffic was at a standstill. A replica of John Lennon's psychedelic Rolls-Royce cruised the streets. Fans took pictures on the famous zebra crossing, and popular tribute artists impersonating the Fab Four re-created the scene. And for a schoolteacher from Essex, England, it's a day she'll never forget.

When Lindsay Humphreys (Kane) and her family got out of the St. John's Wood tube station, there was a sea of people. There were police were on hand to keep people moving. Lindsay ended up at the back of the crowd. Her mother found sanctuary by sitting on a park bench and chatting with other fans. But her sister grabbed her arm and made sure Lindsay was down front.

Meanwhile, Paul impersonator Joe Kane had to keep walking

Joe Kane dressed as barefoot Paul on the Abbey Road zebra crossing, surrounded by "George," "John," and "Ringo" and crowd, down on one knee
proposing to Lindsay Humphreys on August 8, 2019.

across and back on the zebra crossing. He was wearing a dark blue suit
just like Paul on that day, and of course he was barefoot. Joe was a bun-
dle of nerves, but not for the reason you may be thinking. Lindsay made
it to the front of the crowd. They locked eyes, and that was it. In front
of the crowds, reporters, and photographers, Joe got down on one knee
and proposed to the love of his life. She said yes, and they sealed it with
a kiss; then he was immediately whisked off into the crowd. Was it all a
dream? Did it really happen? It really did, and the newly engaged couple
celebrated in style later that evening. The next day the engagement photos made the national papers. There was even a YouTube video marking
the moment.

"Of all the proposals, nothing beats that," Lindsay Kane, said. "Especially for a Beatles fan." She jokes that this was her 15 minutes of fame.

Like most of our couples in this chapter, it all started at International Beatleweek in Liverpool. In August 2011, Lindsay was at the Cavern Pub—across the street from the Cavern Club—watching Revolver, a tribute band from Scotland. Joe, who was also in a Scottish tribute band called Them Beatles, was watching the show as well.

"He wasn't dressed up as Paul McCartney; he was there as a fan like me," Lindsay said. "When he spoke to me, I didn't understand his accent very well."

They muddled through, and Lindsay understood enough to know they had lots in common. Especially the Beatles. They both had watched *The Beatles Anthology* and *Backbeat*—the movie about Stuart Sutcliff and Astrid Kirchherr—and had the same books and albums. It wasn't only a Beatles match; they had other things in common as well. "We liked each other," Lindsay said simply.

When the magical week was over Joe went to South Africa with his band, where he played Paul; she went back to her teaching job in Essex. They kept in touch for a year and planned to meet up the same time the

Zebra crossing post-proposal hug, Joe Kane, still on one knee, and Lindsay Humphreys, on August 8, 2019.

95

following year at the next International Beatleweek. This time he invited her up to Glasgow, Scotland, where he lived, and his band was playing a gig. It was quite a big trip for our schoolteacher, who had never been farther north than Liverpool.

"When I got there all the other bandmembers' girlfriends [now wives] were there to meet me at the station. I was part of the gang right away."

Feeling right at home, in 2013 Lindsay moved to Glasgow. In July 2021 they were married. The wedding, originally planned for June 27, 2020, was postponed due to the COVID-19 pandemic. The new date, July 10, 2021, just so happened to be Beatles Day in the United Kingdom. It was meant to be. Them Beatles, which included Clark Gilmour, disbanded in 2015 but reunited for the occasion. They also played at Michael and Melanie Holt's wedding, a couple you will meet later in this chapter.

"The Beatles played a massive part in both our lives," Lindsay said. "If I hadn't gotten into The Beatles and gone to Beatleweek, I wouldn't have met Joe." At 40, Lindsay is a second-generation fan and was introduced to the band by her parents, but she gives her mother most of the credit. Her mom saw The Beatles in concert twice in London in 1963 and 1964. Her dad saw them "only" once in 1964. It was her mom who took her to see *Backbeat* when she was 13, and she couldn't take her eyes off The Beatles tearing up the stage in Hamburg.

"When we got home, she [her mom] got all her vinyl Beatles records out. I saw the *Hard Day's Night* cover, and nothing was ever the same again."

To solidify Lindsay's love, her mom took her to see the tribute band Bootleg Beatles every year at Albert Hall in London. In 2006 Lindsay went to her first International Beatleweek.

Lindsay's favorite Beatle is John, but her mom is hooked on Paul.

"When I told her Joe plays Paul in a tribute band, she was very impressed," Lindsay said. "Joe is a great Paul. He plays all the guitars and equipment and wears all the costumes. He even learned to play bass left-handed like Paul."

All his hard work paid off. There was a time when Joe was still dressed after a show and two older women in an elevator said, "Ooh, Paul McCartney." Once he was playing in France, and there was a girl talking to him like he was actually Paul McCartney, Lindsay said.

The couple has a dedicated Beatles room in their home, and you can always hear Beatles music wafting through the walls. They watched

Peter Jackson's *Get Back* documentary together three times through, and they're not done yet.

"The Beatles are a special bond for us. We have an international Beatle family at Beatleweek," Lindsay said.

Lindsay is not only an art teacher; she is also an artist who loves making Beatles-related pieces. She made a replica of George Harrison's psychedelic guitar.

Joe has taken his talent for Beatles music to a new level. Just like Paul McCartney, Joe wrote, recorded, and played all the instruments on his album *Hits to Spare*. He produced the record at Fabbey Road, better known as the couple's garage, in the span of two months from December 2020 through January 2021. The album is all original songs that are upbeat and have a familiarity with and the heart of the early Beatles. It's really quite astounding, in my opinion. The album sold very well, especially in Japan. Now, Joe is beginning to tour and promote the album with his new band Poppermost. Lindsay got into the act by taking the album cover photo.

Could it be possible that in 50 years we'll be celebrating that album cover photo? Tomorrow never knows.

Maybe He's Amazed

They met at Beatleweek, then honeymooned
among their Beatles friends.

She was entranced while he played "Maybe I'm Amazed," her favorite song. The guitar solo ended, and suddenly the whole room was quiet. She couldn't imagine why. He looked down from the stage right at her.

"Will you marry me?" he asked.

I must be dreaming, she thought. It took a moment for the words to sink in. Finally, she jumped onstage and shouted "Yes!" The entire room cheered.

It wasn't Paul McCartney proposing to Nancy. It was Beatles superfan Michael Holt, playing with the tribute band Them Beatles, proposing to the superfan love of his life, Melanie, at International Beatleweek in August 2013. They married the following August and shared the honeymoon suite at the Hard Days Night Hotel during that year's Beatleweek.

The couple sounded like lovestruck teens when—on speakerphone from their home in Hednesford, England, 86 miles north of Liverpool—they described the romance that sprang from their mutual love for the band and their annual Beatleweek pilgrimage.

Michael and Melanie Holt with exuberant smiles after their wedding ceremony in August 2014. The two met during International Beatleweek in Liverpool.

Mel's heart went boom when Mike crossed that room, but still he was quite an imposing figure, standing 6'4". He was tall, dark, and handsome, but she was quite shy and didn't say a word the first time they met in 1998, her fourth annual Beatleweek excursion.

Mel didn't know that Mike was gobsmacked as well. "She was beautiful, charismatic, and a great dancer. She had a great sense of humor, that was clear, and a great personality," Mike gushed. But just like Mel, he was too shy to introduce himself. They had friends in common, but they didn't speak a word to each other. Mike simply hoped he would see Mel the next year and vowed that he would summon up his courage to talk to her by then.

Mike didn't go back to Beatleweek for many years. Mel didn't know what happened. In 2010 the two met up for the second time, and Mike knew he had to get her into his life. What started as an innocent long-distance email friendship quickly blossomed into a romance. Mike didn't want to waste another minute. He moved to northern England, and then came the perfect proposal.

The wedding guests were all their Beatles friends. "All You Need Is Love" serenaded them as they left the chapel, and they drove off to their Beatleweek honeymoon in a 1960s Volkswagen camper.

Mel is a devout Paul fan; Mike is just as devoted to John. Marriage takes compromise, the couple jokes, and they have compromised on George. "It actually works quite well," Mel said. "The pieces fit together."

You could say it was fate that drew them together.

The first memory Mel has of Paul McCartney is seeing a televised concert on BBC-TV called *From Rio to Liverpool*. Mike was at that concert. He was 18 and had taken a Cavern City Tours coach trip to see Paul McCartney live in Hamburg. The first time Mel saw Paul McCartney in person was at a concert in 1990 in what was then the Echo Arena on Kings Dock in Liverpool. Mike was there sitting in the same section, but the two hadn't yet met. "It's the weird things life throws you," Mike said.

Now they enjoy Beatles events together: Paul McCartney concerts, countless trips to Liverpool for every Beatles anniversary or birthday, and, of course, Beatleweek. While in Liverpool, they have done the National Trust tours of John's and Paul's childhood homes several times, finding something new each time. They often travel to London just to take a Beatles walking tour, which includes of course the famous Abbey Road crosswalk. Their love for the lads doesn't stop when they get home. You can find them at the local pub enjoying a local band playing Beatles music. Or you might find them cozied up on the couch watching Beatles films or listening to the music.

"He loves John, and I love Paul," Mel said. "We would be happy to listen to both all day if we could."

For both, their obsession started in their teenage years. Mel became a massive fan the first time she heard Paul's album *Give My Regards to Broad Street*. She watched Wings videos on *Top of the Pops*.

"As music declined in the late 1980s, I thought *there's got to be something better*," Mel said. She bought the Red (*Beatles 1962–1966*) and Blue (*Beatles 1967–1970*) Albums. She was hooked—hook, line, and sinker. She bought every album, poster, and book she could find and watched every film. She changed from eating right-handed to left-handed to be like Paul and was a vegetarian for 11 years, following her idol. She lived in Liverpool for 4 years, attending university there. Later, she found her tribe in a small fan club of 12 girls called the Liverscruffs.

"They follow Paul around to different things around the country and scream," Mike said kindheartedly.

When the Liverpool Institute of Performing Arts (LIPA), which Paul cofounded in 1996, first opened and Paul and Queen Elizabeth were there, "so were we," Mel said. "When Paul got his knighthood, we watched him going in and going out."

Mike joked that he had to get Mel away from the screaming Liverscruffs at Beatleweek to get a word in edgewise.

Mike was raised by his grandparents due to his parents' divorce. He was 14 when he went to see his dad with a Depeche Mode single in his hand. His dad played it, said it was good, and then said, "Listen to this!" He played "Strawberry Fields" on his state-of-the-art stereo system and turned it up loud. It was all around the room.

"It was the most amazing thing I'd ever heard," Mike said. He brought the Blue Album home and played it for his grandfather. His grandfather said that The Beatles were always good. "That helped me on my way to my obsession," Mike said. "The music was something everybody loved. It wasn't just a teenage thing."

That was the start. He watched *The Compleat Beatles* documentary on VHS, then, like Mel, started collecting everything he could, especially records and posters. He took out books from the library about The Beatles and renewed them time and time again, never able to get enough. He watched George and John on videos too, and George inspired him to learn guitar. "George was so cool and such a great guitarist," Mike said. "Sometimes watching George play guitar can make me cry."

Both collectors, Mike and Mel each had doubles and triples of everything when they got together. In the end they gave quite a bit of it away to friends and kept one spare copy of everything. But they still have 10 copies of *Band on the Run*.

Their home is a tasteful shrine. "You know we're fans because we have our box sets and a few other things on display," Mel said. But they keep it low-key. "We don't want people to be scared when they walk in."

It was a long and winding road getting the two of them together. Mike said that he wishes he'd had the gumption to speak to Mel that first time they met. "But that may not have been the right time," Mike mused philosophically. "It's the twists and turns life takes you. It might have gone another way. This is the way it was meant to be."

The Best George Double and His Beautiful Spanish Wife

He gazed down from the stage right into my eyes. Did he really? Wasn't it his job to make every woman feel he was singing just to her? But I could swear he was watching me dance. Not really dancing as much as becoming the music. He smiled that million-dollar smile. He wiggled, just a little; if you blinked, you would have missed it. He moved his eyebrows up and down in that special George way.

I was in heaven. There was nowhere else I would have rather been than where I was right at that moment: the Cavern Club in Liverpool. I knew it wasn't really him. He'd been gone for nearly 20 years. But this was the young version of him, the version I have loved for as long as I can remember. Whoever it was that was on that stage looked, sounded, and acted like him. He embodied his essence, and he was smiling at me! In an instant I was 16.

Years later back in New York, I discovered that dream's real identity. I spoke to him and his beautiful Spanish wife about the love that had bloomed between them at the Cavern Club in Liverpool. I must

Paul and Meri Jones in December 2019, in front of the psychedelic car they drove away in on their wedding day.

admit I was nervous and blushing as we spoke, relieved that it was a transatlantic call and he couldn't see my face. His adorable Liverpudlian accent and his friendly demeanor kept the dream alive. I wasn't crushed—okay, maybe a little—when I spoke to his beautiful bride and discovered they'd been married for only a few months. I was happy for them both. After all, it was just a fantasy.

His real name is Paul Jones, and he plays the best George I have ever seen, in the Cavern Club Beatles, the house band at the Cavern Club in Liverpool—and as the kids say, in my humble opinion, the best tribute band in the world. He is also assistant director of Cavern City Tours. His bride, Meritxell—Meri, from Barcelona—was a bartender at the same club trying to improve her English. The two worked in the same place at the same time for years, but their paths didn't cross. He was in front of the footlights, and she was behind the bar.

"When I saw him, I said, 'Oh, he's cute,'" Meri said in her exotic Spanish/Liverpudlian accent. "You see him and you think he's shy. But he's so good on the mic. He's always welcoming and happy. He's the best George I've ever seen!"

When Paul would come to the bar with the other guys from the business side of things every Friday night, the bar crew were on their best behavior. These businessmen held their jobs in their hands. Paul was always nice, said hi, and asked everyone their names, Meri said.

"The minute she started working there, everyone was aware of her," Paul said. "She's incredibly beautiful."

Paul was having a drink at the Cavern Pub—across the street from the Cavern Club—when Meri came in after her shift one night. In his usual manner, Paul started a conversation with her. "After about a half an hour, I knew I was in trouble," he said happily.

They got married with all their Cavern friends in attendance at the Liverpool Town Hall in December 2019. It's the same place where the famous picture was taken of The Beatles waving off a balcony when they returned to Liverpool for the premiere of *A Hard Day's Night*.

It was a long and winding international road that brought this Beatles-loving couple together.

Paul is a Liverpool native who grew up in a home full of musicians. Beatles music wafted through the walls of his childhood home through speakers and live on the guitars his family played. Paul has played Beatles music on his guitar practically since birth.

Back in Barcelona, Meri was growing up as the only child of a father who is a rock-and-roll enthusiast, collector, and journalist. He has a radio show and loves anything American or British, especially The Beatles. Meri has seen every big name in concert and went to her first International Beatle-week with her father when she was just seven years old.

"The first time I went to Liverpool, I didn't know anything about The Beatles," she said. "They were fascinating, and I don't know why. It was a tale; The Beatles were a story. My dad started telling me about John, Paul, George, and Ringo, how they met and all the rest. It was so exciting, I wanted to know more. It led to my curiosity, and I started learning the language through the songs."

Paul and Meri Jones onstage at the Cavern Club on their wedding day, December 2019.

At the same time in Liverpool, Paul was 12 when he started his first band. To get rehearsals going they would play Beatles music, the same way The Beatles would play Chuck Berry and Elvis to get warmed up. When Paul (Jones) was 15, his band had its first gig as The Beat Beatles. They won a contest, and when he was 16 they were on TV.

Paul took his talent and attended LIPA, which was cofounded by Paul McCartney. At 21, Paul Jones graduated with honors with a degree in sound engineering. Paul McCartney attends every LIPA graduation and hands each student their diploma. Paul Jones shook hands with Paul McCartney. "My dad climbed over four people to shake hands with

Paul," Paul Jones said. "I was like 'Dad, sit down; don't embarrass me.' But he did get to shake his hand."

Meanwhile in Barcelona, Meri went to Beatleweek every year with her dad. She fell in love with Liverpool. She always had a great time and came back gushing to her friends. Finally, at 18 she left her dad behind and went to Liverpool with her best friend. She loved it so much that she decided to move there. Her dad knew people at the Cavern, and she got a job behind the bar.

After graduation Paul worked on cruise ships as John Lennon, which allowed him to travel around the world and bring Beatles music wherever he went. Four years later, the Cavern Club officially put together a Beatles band. "They needed a George, and I didn't think I could do it. I never played much lead guitar," Paul said humbly. "Tony [Paul McCartney in the band] said to learn 'Roll Over Beethoven' and tell them you know the other ones. I got the part, and I had to learn all the songs."

"He's the best George I've ever seen," Meri said. "My dad loves George, and he thinks so too. When he calls us now, he says, 'How's Paul?' And I say, 'He's fine, Dad, and I'm fine too!'"

Meri doesn't play an instrument, but that hasn't stopped her from joining in the fun. "She has a beautiful voice," Paul said. She has become Linda in their Paul McCartney and Wings shows.

Meri speaks lovely English and said she owes it all to The Beatles. "Their accents are so easy," she said. "And their songs are so happy."

Paul and Meri are very happily fixtures in the Liverpool Beatles scene.

She Saw a Photograph—Oh Boy

Paul McCartney was born in the Old Walton Hospital in Liverpool in June 1942. Exactly five years later, lifelong fan Colin Eaton was born in the same hospital. Paul's mother, Mary, was a maternity ward nurse at the same hospital prior to these momentous occasions. The hospital closed its doors in 2010, and in 2011 it was converted into a residential community.

That's where Beatle fanatics Colin and Katie Eaton live now. The couple got married on July 7, 2016, Ringo's 76th birthday. They say that these are both serendipitous coincidences.

This late-in-life pair met at the Casbah Coffee Club during

International Beatleweek in 2009. The Casbah Club, as it was known in its heyday, ran from 1959 to 1962 in a basement in West Derby, a suburb of Liverpool. It was owned and operated by Mona, the mother of the original Beatles drummer Pete Best. The Beatles were in on the ground floor—so to speak—of the club, decorating, painting, and sprucing it up before it opened. Paul McCartney famously said it was "their" club.

The Beatles, young and rough before Brian Epstein and before the Cavern Club, played regularly at the Casbah Club with Pete on drums. Now it's a hidden gem for fans.

In 2009, Katie traveled 5,000 miles from her home in Oakland, California, for her annual pilgrimage to Beatleweek. More than a fan, she is a well-known historian and writer for Beatlenews.com. She started writing because she wanted to be a fly on the wall for fans who couldn't be at the exciting events she had the privilege of attending, such as Beatleweek, the Fest for Beatle Fans in New York, and concerts by Paul and Ringo. At these events, she heard fascinating speakers who were Beat-les insiders and gave glimpses into stories that weren't in any books, and she wanted to spread the news in her articles.

That day, Katie was listening to Beatles music live at the Casbah for the first time. She was enthralled by the sights and sounds. Colin, a native Liverpudlian, was on hand taking pictures for a charity. He noticed Katie right off. "It was love at first sight for me," he happily said. She was wearing hand-painted "hippie" pants. He mustered the courage to approach her and say "Cool pants."

"I thought he was quite a strong character,"

Katie and Colin Hickox Eaton at International Beatleweek, August 2019. Katie moved across the pond from America to be with her Beatles sweetheart.

Katie said. "He was bald with a big grin, and he was a nice person. I never in my wildest dreams thought anything more would happen."

When Colin gave her a ride into downtown Liverpool, "it was one of those future moments," Katie said. "I had one foot in the car and one foot out of the car. The stars aligned. There was the spark of a romance, and I realized then that something might happen in the future."

They exchanged email addresses with the promise of photos to come. That started a seven-year courtship that spanned two continents. Hopelessly romantic, Colin sent Katie poetry every Sunday. She swooned, and the two racked up their share of frequent flyer miles.

They got married at St. George's Hall in Liverpool in 2016, right across the street from the Lime Street station where she would take the train into town to meet Colin. Jon Keats, better known as John Lennon in tribute bands, walked her down the aisle. Jon and another John Lennon, Clark Gilmour, played "All You Need Is Love" and "Here Comes the Sun" during the ceremony. Their reception was at the Cavern Club, where the groom picked up his guitar and played, with all their Beatles friends cheering.

Katie is a bigger fan than Colin, delving into the band's hidden story and keeping up with the twists and turns life dealt each Beatle. But Colin humbly talks about the day he met all four lads backstage at a gig in the Grafton Ballroom in 1963. There were lots of bands on the bill, and Colin's brother, Barry, was a drummer in the Dominant Four, an opening act. Barry took his little brother Colin, 16 at the time, backstage.

"He introduced me," Colin said. "He said, 'Guys, this is my little brother.' A couple of them were smoking. One looked up and said hi, but they really just chatted with each other about band stuff." That's all Colin had to say about that clandestine meeting with the biggest band in history.

As Katie was telling me the story of her obsession over the intercontinental phone call, I could hear Colin tinkering with "Paperback Writer" on his guitar, the perfect backdrop for her story.

Katie loved The Beatles long before she even knew who they were. When she was growing up, the boys next door would play Beatles records "really loud" when their parents weren't home. Katie would go running to the side of the house where the windows were open and she could hear the music best. She would dance all night—at three years old.

Katie says she's not obsessed. She never had a favorite Beatle but instead looked at all of them as a unit. She had a troubled childhood, and their music and pictures of all four of them would make her feel better. "They were part of my emotional support system," she said.

Thirty years later, Katie did more than look at pictures. "As I approached my 40s, I realized how much I didn't know," she said. Fortunately, she had the time and money to go to Liverpool and discovered her first annual Beatleweek in 2001. She felt inspired, amazed, and privileged. She's never missed a year since then except in 2020, when it didn't happen because of the worldwide pandemic. She read books too and discovered there was an entire history behind the band.

The more Katie read, the more questions she had. She started to get glimpses of the story behind the story told in bits and pieces from people who were there with the lads. She related to John, who in her opinion was the most troubled. She tried to learn everything about him. Even Katie and Colin's first meeting at the Casbah was related to John: it was a childhood friend of John's who asked Colin to take photographs.

Through John, Katie discovered the fascinating story of Beatles' manager Brian Epstein, who is a huge figure in the band's history. Little was known about him until recently, with a new biopic and a new TV series in development. Katie dug into his story, which has led to her lending a Brian Epstein exhibit to The Beatles Story museum in Liverpool. Items include a picture of handwritten lyrics from when Brian attempted to write a song for the boys. Frustrated, he ripped it up and threw it away, but his chauffeur picked it out of the trash and taped it back together. There are also press clippings and a letter from Brian to The Beatles.

Katie's byline reads "Katie Hickox" in the articles she has written, and she has dedicated her life to raising awareness of the little-known facts about The Beatles. She says that being an American in Liverpool is a novelty, and Liverpudlians want to hear the story of why she crossed the pond. "Many people from Liverpool are tired of hearing about The Beatles," she said. "But then they meet me, and I change their lives. I make them realize The Beatles helped to make the world a better place. They influenced me, and it shows in the way I live my life."

Katie works in information technology support for the National Health System. "What I do supports the NHS nursing staff, people who in turn help them [the people of Liverpool]. Living in Liverpool, you almost always meet someone who knew someone who had gone to school with or who got to see The Beatles play at a local club," Katie said. "I'm always learning something new."

There's no doubt the couple are fans when you walk into their shrine of a home. Their love of the Beatles is larger than life, with three-foot cardboard cutouts of John talking to Paul and a tea towel in the kitchen with a picture of The Beatles from *The Ed Sullivan Show* with their mouths open, singing. Also proudly displayed is a photograph of George at a press conference with Brian in the background, and posters cover the walls like wallpaper.

Talking to the happy pair—Colin, 73, and Katie, 60—made me feel happy inside. They are living proof that all you need is love.

FIVE

The DJs Who Keep the Records Spinning

Where would we be without the DJs who spin the tunes that help keep the boys in the forefront? From SiriusXM's Beatles Channel to *Breakfast with The Beatles* to a Beatles aficionado at a public radio station in New York City, these people keep the band playing on.

Peter Asher

Peter Asher generously invited me into his beautiful beachfront home in southern California and offered me a cup of tea. As we sat in his lovely kitchen with his three dogs milling around, the comfortable setting felt as if I was meeting an old friend instead of conducting an interview. And oh, the stories this friend could tell.

As Beatles fans, we know Peter as Jane Asher's brother. For those who don't know, Jane was Paul's first fiancée. We also know Peter as the man who tells those wonderful inside stories about The Beatles on his show *Peter Asher: From Me to You* on the Beatles Channel. He has written a book around those stories called *The Beatles: A to Zed*, published in 2019 and in its third printing.

Some of those stories come from the two years when Paul McCartney famously lived in the Ashers' home with Peter, Jane, their sister Clare, and their parents. Paul lived in the bedroom next to Peter on the top floor of the six-story house from late 1963 to 1965 during the five-year period he was dating Jane. There's that side to Peter, and then there's so much more. His own vast music career includes being half of the popular acoustic duo Peter and Gordon, from the 1960s. After performing for years, he became a Grammy Award–winning record producer and president of his own talent management agency, Peter Asher Management, based in southern California. His producing career

The author and Peter Asher in his southern California kitchen, February 22, 2022.

includes albums for music icons such as James Taylor, whose career he launched when he gave him his first recording contract with Apple Records; Diana Ross; Cher; Kenny Loggins; the Dixie Chicks; 10,000 Manias; and our favorite drummer, Ringo Starr. Peter's management roster past and present includes Linda Ronstadt, Joni Mitchell, Randy Newman, Carole King, and again James Taylor.

Even knowing all this, I sat in his kitchen with my voice recorder on waiting to hear stories about our boys that only Peter could tell. He was happy to oblige.

Peter's room was right next to Paul's on the upper level of his family's home. Music was always wafting through the walls of Paul's room. Sometimes Paul was working out songs on his guitar, and other times he was playing his favorite bands on his record player. Peter was always playing his music too, and very often they were listening to the same bands.

Let's pick up the needle and start this song at the beginning. How did Paul end up living with Peter? The connection, of course, is Peter's sister Jane. In 1963 Beatlemania was already at a frenzied pitch in England. The four lads were sharing a flat in the Mayfair district of London, on the West End. They had a Green Street address, which wasn't too far from the Ashers' house on Wimpole Street. At that point, Paul and Jane were dating pretty seriously.

"It was chaos—four successful young guys sharing a flat," Peter recalled. "He was over at my house a lot. He was crazy about my sister, but also I think he liked that it was a pretty organized household. My mother was a remarkable woman, and he got on well with all of us, so he would come over for dinner or bring his laundry or whatever—the way boyfriends do. Eventually, our parents offered him the guest room. He ended up not just using it occasionally. He moved in there for two years."

That was the point when Peter and Paul became fast friends. They were both quite young, Peter being about 19 or 20 and Paul only 21.

"If you're living next door to someone and sharing a bathroom, and you're both interested in music and you both have record collections and guitars and stuff, you become friends."

I was trying to imagine what it was like having Paul around the house. What did he like to do on a quiet Tuesday night? What did he watch on TV? What did he like to eat? Peter couldn't put his finger on those details because he said there was very little downtime. By then Peter and Gordon had a gig every night, which Paul went to a couple of times. And of course, our Paul was skyrocketing to the stars. "I don't remember ever sitting around with nothing to do and saying 'Hey, let's go to the movies.' But we occasionally went out to clubs together. I remember going with him to see the Rolling Stones at the Scene Club. We went to the Ad Lib Club or Dolly's. They were the places that knew how to treat celebrities."

The Scene, the Ad Lib Club, and Dolly's Nightclub were some of The Beatles' favorite haunts on the swinging London scene. They had their own table at the Ad Lib Club, and that's where they went after the premiere of *A Hard Day's Night*. It was in that club where Ringo proposed to Maureen. Dolly's Nightclub was quite popular as well and often hosted The Beatles, the Rolling Stones, and other luminaries.

When they weren't clubbing, there was, of course, a lot of music being written in that house. Paul famously gave Peter and Gordon their first hit record with the song "A World Without Love." It was credited to Lennon–McCartney, as all their songs were no matter who wrote them. Paul knew that the song wasn't quite right for The Beatles and offered it to Peter and Gordon, who knew there was no possibility they would turn it down. It catapulted the duo to number one on the UK charts and

111

actually knocked "Can't Buy Me Love" out of the number one spot after it solidly topped the charts for many weeks.

Peter's mother Margaret was a musician and a music professor—oboe teacher at the Guildhall School of Music and Dance. She had a small music room downstairs in the basement where she occasionally gave private oboe lessons. There was a small upright piano, a small music stand and a two-person sofa. History was made there the day Paul and John wrote "I Want to Hold Your Hand" in that room, and Peter was the first to hear it!

"I was upstairs," Peter said. "My mother told him he could use that piano [in the basement] any time he wanted to. John came over and they went down there together. Interestingly, with no guitars. The guitars were upstairs. Paul called up to me after a couple of hours and asked me if I wanted to hear the song they just finished. So, I came downstairs, and they played it! I thought it was brilliant! I thought it was remarkable! I immediately asked them to play it again, which, of course, is a natural reaction to the sign of a hit record. By the same token, they were equally delighted to play it again." And we, as fans, have been playing it ever since.

It wasn't often that Paul worked on songs in front of Peter, but those are moments Peter remembers well. One of those times was when Paul was working on "I'm Looking Through You."

"I remember him working on the bridge of that song one day. It's one of the only ones I remember him working on actually in front of me. 'Love has a nasty habit of disappearing overnight'—he was working on that line," Peter said.

"I remember him playing 'Fool on the Hill' when it was written because I was impressed by the fact that he not only had the song worked out but the arrangement done in his head, what the flutes and recorder and stuff were going to be playing. He was explaining some of that and singing it. My parents were there too. We were on the big piano in the sitting room downstairs when he played that."

Unbeknownst to Peter at the time, he had some influence on "Norwegian Wood," or at least his furniture did. And, he says, the real meaning to the line "so I lit a fire" is quite astonishing.

"Paul attributed the Norwegian Wood to some pine in my bedroom," Peter said. "I had some shelves, but I never had paneling. Paul did say in some interview that it wasn't really Norwegian Wood it was pine, and it was based on something in my bedroom. I had pine shelves so maybe that was it, but Norwegian Wood is a lot more poetic.

Apparently, the wood in my room had something to do with the invention of the song—even though it's primarily a John song, . . . the Norwegian Wood may have come from Paul."

Let's talk about when John sings "So, I lit a fire. Isn't it good? Norwegian wood?"

"It sounded to me like was arson in the end," Peter said. "But some people have said, 'no it meant he was lighting a fire in the fireplace or smoking a joint,' this, that, and the other. There are all sorts of interpretations. But I'm certain the setting fire to the house is the correct interpretation."

You may have heard the tale of how "Yesterday" came to be. But did you know that when Paul awoke from a dream with the melody to "Yesterday" in his head, he was living with the Ashers' house? He got out of bed, quickly went to the piano and found the chords. He played it for everyone he knew, bandmates and friends, because he was sure this was a tune he had heard before. Everyone assured him they had never heard it, and indeed it turned out that the music was his. The very first person he asked if she had ever heard the tune before was Peter and Jane's mum, Margaret. She was the first to utter the words that this just might be an original, and then he was off on his journey. Months later he finished what might be one of the biggest hits of all time, "Yesterday."

Paul respected the Ashers' opinions so much that in 1967—two years after he moved out—as soon as "Sgt. Pepper" was finished, he brought the new recording over to their house.

"He had an acetate they just cut, just put it all together, assembled all the different songs together. He played [it] for the family. It sounded amazing. You realized right away it was breaking new ground, the way everything joined up. That's why it was significant that he just brought it on the day they just finished editing all that together, and it was remarkable."

It was their ability to create characters in their songs that is one of the things that impresses Peter the most about their songwriting.

"They were writing songs about imaginary people and making up stories, like 'She's Leaving Home.' It's a movie script—it's a short story. It's got dialogue. That's pretty extraordinary. It's a different kind of songwriting. They would think of new angles for songs. Even going back to 'She Loves You.' It's not an I Love You, You Love Me, song; it's reportage. It's something different. Lyrically they grew more complex as time went on. Their imagination grew. In addition, they invent characters and stories and imaginary situations. Mysterious fools on the hill.

They're extremely creative, each of them and both of them—together or separately and George. Specifically miraculous inventions."

Of course, The Beatles' music changed throughout their career, but there are no great artists in history that don't change. They changed in the same way that if you're a painter you go from the blue period to another period and head in different directions. They got more complicated and brought more into their music.

"They incorporated things they'd always loved. John's love of Lewis Carroll and his slightly surreal writing was no doubt present from the beginning of their career, but gradually bits of that became incorporated into his thinking, and suddenly you've got, 'I Am the Walrus' or 'Lucy in the Sky with Diamonds.' They recognized gradually that you could incorporate everything you heard and everything you knew into what you were writing and singing and give us the benefit. Every album changed and got a little bit more complicated. A little bit more interesting. At the same time, I'm not saying they were better. Because you go back and listen to "I Want to Hold Your Hand,' it's hard to imagine anything better than that at all. Great artists always change."

Around that same time period as the release of "Sgt. Pepper" and soon after their beloved manager Brian Epstein died, they were told they had a lot of money and maybe they should start an enterprise to diminish the amount of tax they owed. That was when Apple Corps was formed. Peter was in on the ground floor.

"It was Paul's idea. [He] liked the idea of starting a venture that was more generous and more willing to listen than record companies were in that era. Record companies were very formal enterprises back then. They looked upon pop music as a necessary evil to pay for classical music and everything that was their God-given duty. Paul decided that they should start not just a record company but an entertainment company. Films, television, books, electronics, strangely clothing and eventually much of which turned out to be a bit of a mistake. But musically the idea was they would listen while the big record companies didn't. The head of EMI was Sir Joseph Lockwood, and when you went into his office you felt like you should be bowing; it was that sort of a thing. Paul wanted to get rid of that and make it much more accessible, which he did. We took an ad saying 'send us your music, we will listen.' We got nothing through the send-in process. It was all disappointing. We got pages of lyrics that didn't even scan that someone was certain John Lennon was going to write music for. You couldn't even imagine how bad some of the stuff was. It was a bit depressing. We discovered people in different ways. Each one would be quite different."

It was indeed a much more serendipitous way that Peter Asher discovered James Taylor, one of the first artists he signed to Apple Records as head of artists and repertoire (A&R).

The connection started many years before the two actually met, back when Peter and Gordon were touring in America. The duo were given different bands as opening acts by the powers that be. One of those bands was the King Bees. Peter became friends with the band's guitar player, Danny Kortchmar. They stayed in touch after the duo's touring years were over. When the King Bees disbanded, Danny joined a New York–based band called the Flying Machine with his childhood friend, James Taylor.

"They had no money, bad management, and their record company disappeared," Peter said. "The band broke up. James decided to go to London. Danny gave him my phone number. He said, 'Look, here's one of my best friends. I used to play with him. He okay. He's in London; call him up.'"

James did just that. When he introduced himself as Danny Kortchmar's friend, Peter invited him over. James played some songs for Peter, and Peter "went crazy."

"I told him they were great. I explained to him that I just got this new job as head of A&R for a record label and that I could sign people and would he like a record contract. He said yes, please, he'd love one. I explained whose label it was and so on. So, within two days of arriving there he was in Apple meeting Paul and George, and we signed him up!" Peter produced James's first album, and Paul and George played on a couple of tunes.

Director of A&R was not the first job Peter was offered at Apple, but it was not long until he got there.

When Paul first started talking about the idea of Apple Corps, he asked Peter to produce some records for Apple because he knew Peter wanted to be a producer and was already producing things. "In fact, the first record I ever produced, he played drums on." So, it began with Paul asking Peter to produce. As Apple Records became real, Paul said he needed somebody to be head of A&R and asked Peter if he would do it.

"I said, 'Yes! Of course!' What could be better than working for a cool new record label and specifically working for The Beatles? I thought that was supercool. I accepted. It was a bit chaotic, but there were some great people working there. Derek Taylor became a great friend of mine—who I had met before but didn't know very well. He was sort of The Beatles' PR person and all-around artistic guide. He was a genius. Peter Brown, who was The Beatles' right-hand man, I liked a lot. We hired this guy Ron Kass to be head of the label itself business-wise. He was the head of Liberty Records in America or had been, and he had a very good résumé in that regard. He was also married to Joan Collins, which we thought was incredibly cool. It was great! We began in Baker Street at first and then Widmore Street and finally Saville Row. My office in Saville Row was the top left as you look at the building. Derek Taylor's office was on the third floor I think, then Peter Brown below which is where The Beatles had an office too. It was great. It was an unusual company, and people forget that in the end we did make some good records. We put some records out and had some hits. It worked. It was when they got a bit beyond their original ambitions or perhaps fulfilled their original ambitions too much. It did start getting into the clothing business and the electronics business and all this other stuff. That's when things went a bit awry. It did end up with overspending and craziness, which is why they decided they needed to bring in something of a tough guy to be in charge of the whole venture, not just the record company, and that was, of course, Allen Klein. Which is when I left."

Speaking of Apple Corps, this seemed like the perfect time to ask Peter his impression of the *Get Back* docuseries, which I was happy to hear he enjoyed very much.

"The first one [the original film made from the 60 hours of footage, *Let It Be*] created a bleaker picture than I recall, but I wasn't in the studio. I was never at Twickenham. I was in the basement once or twice, but I wasn't there for the rooftop concert even though people still occasionally tell me that I was. I wasn't. That's when I was in America," Peter said.

"The first one emphasized the arguments of it. I remember some rows—I wasn't there for the stuff they were filming, but I do remember some other arguments in Peter Brown's office and stuff like that. But when they were working on their own music it was the collaborative stuff you see in the current movie. I remember it as being entirely correct."

From the very beginning Peter was very impressed by The Beatles. He was impressed with their songwriting talent, their enthusiasm and their stage presence.

In the early days, Peter and Gordon toured with The Beatles in Germany for a week. That's the only time he was onstage with them and watched them live, but that certainly was enough to know they were genius. It was when he accompanied them to a BBC broadcast where there was no audience that he realized how powerful their sound really was.

"You could really hear them, totally clearly. It was a bit like the studio, but it's a live broadcast so they're all playing and singing at once. That was really impressive partly because of how loud they were. They sang really loud, I guess because [of] all that practice in German clubs. When Gordon and I were having it easy in a bar or a coffeeshop playing our folky guitars without even microphones, they were compelled to scream and yell in these German clubs and the result was ... the power of their singing and the togetherness of their singing, which was just a function of massive amounts of practice. They were impressive memories because they did play and sing very well and very together even when they couldn't hear each other, which is not easy to do."

There are almost no words to describe the magic of the four Beatles together.

"One of the miracles of The Beatles was that they were incredibly helpful to each other in identifying their own strengths and weaknesses. As great as solo Beatles stuff is—there's a certain transcendental greatness that comes from all four of them together interfering with each other's work and making it better and annoying each other in the process no doubt, but that's what groups do. That's why all bands end up to some degree or another getting into arguments. But, of course, once they were free to go unfettered in their own direction, whether it's John making unlistenable music with Yoko or it's George going all Indian, which was happening, of course, before they broke up—their music was freed up in some respects from the necessity of pleasing each other, and they were a difficult audience to please, I have no doubt. The collaboration was as remarkable as they were individually. It couldn't last forever, and it didn't. But we're lucky to have the proceeds of it."

When I asked Peter why The Beatles are still popular 50-plus years on, he looked at me as if I'd lost my mind.

"Why is Bach still popular? Why is Charlie Parker, if you're a jazz fan, or Thelonious Monk still popular? Because they're the best. The Beatles are the best pop music there's ever been. That's why it's not going away. It makes new converts every time people play it to someone. Someone's granny plays a Beatles record, and it changes their life. That's genius. We don't know where that comes from," Peter said.

"There's no band that you can say was as thoroughly mold-breaking as The Beatles since. There have been some colossally good bands and there are now some colossally good bands, but do The Beatles have a current equal? You would have to say no. Will there be bands as big as The Beatles in the future? I hope so."

The Day John Lennon Played DJ on Dennis Elsas's Radio Show

As Beatles fans we know Dennis Elsas as the cohost of the call-in show *The Fab Fourum* on the Beatles Channel. The man with the golden voice is all that and so much more. He is an icon on the New York radio scene, in the business for more than 50 years. As on-air talent, his interviews with Rock Royalty have brought listeners one degree closer to the musicians who play the soundtrack of our lives. His lengthy career started on WNEW-FM in 1971 when progressive FM radio was new.

Dennis Elsas and John Lennon immediately following the 1974 interview on WNEW (photo courtesy Dennis Elsas).

Starting as a fill-in DJ, he quickly moved to full-time music director as well as prolific disc jockey. These days, in addition to his work on the Beatles Channel, he also has shows on Sirius XM's Classic Vinyl channel, and his friendly, comforting voice can be heard on weekday afternoons on New York's public alternative radio station WFUV. But what simply appeals to me about Dennis is his soothing voice that feels like an extra blanket on a cold day.

Dennis has interviewed the giants, including Joni Mitchell, Pete Townshend, Jerry Garcia, and Elton John. But nothing holds a candle to the day John Lennon spent two hours live on air with him on WNEW in 1974. The time was filled with laughter and camaraderie. And it was so much more than a traditional interview. John loved playing DJ; he would read the weather in his own distinct style with his brand of wit thrown in. John even brought some of his own 45s of oldies that he loved and played them on the air. To Dennis's surprise, John was happy to answer questions about his Beatles days. And it was extra special because John had just completed his *Walls and Bridges* album, and the stories he was sharing about it were all brand new.

It was a day Dennis didn't really believe would happen until John and May Pang, his girlfriend during the famous "lost weekend" that lasted 18 months, showed up on the studio's doorstep.

Let's rewind to a couple of weeks earlier when Dennis—who was music director at WNEW at the time—was invited to sit in on John Lennon's recording session at the Record Plant by a friend who worked at Capitol Records. Naturally, Dennis jumped at the opportunity and high-tailed it down to the studios. As he sat in the engineering booth watching John Lennon through the glass, in his head he was screaming *I can't believe I'm watching John Lennon in the studio.* On the outside Dennis was sure to keep his cool. The session drew to a close, and Dennis got to meet May, whom he says couldn't have been nicer. In a "now or never" moment, he threw out the idea of John coming up to the station: "because it couldn't hurt. I said, 'Well, you know if John would ever like to come up to the radio station, we'd love to have him.'" He didn't really expect them to take him up on his offer. At that point, no Beatle had ever been to the station.

Much to Dennis's surprise, May called a couple of weeks later and told him John would love to come. She asked when Dennis would like him. Knowing that he was on the air on Saturday and Sunday afternoons and to be sure he was the DJ at the mic when John Lennon walked in, he said, "How's 4:00 on Saturday?"

"It got arranged very quickly," Dennis said. "I didn't know what to expect. I didn't want to announce it on the air because in those days we didn't to a lot of promos—FM was too hip, too cool. And I didn't believe he was coming, but I did say throughout the afternoon, 'Listen I've got a surprise for you later. I can't say exactly what it is, but tell your friends to turn on the radio.'" So, when John first comes on the air you hear him say "Surprise, surprise. I am Dennis's surprise. It's Dr. Winston O'Boogie at your service." So, he had obviously been hearing me say "I've got a surprise for you."

Starting from the moment John, May, and their friend Richard arrived at the building that housed the station, the event paints a picture of a simpler time. The act of getting into the building on a Saturday in 1974 is a much different picture than how it would go down in 2023.

"There's a long story about the elevator operator—because in an office building on a Saturday in the 1970s there's not that much security. Certainly, nothing like today. There's just a guy that runs the freight elevator. That how things were done in those days. Nobody signed you in. You rang a night bell, someone opened the door, asked where are you going—I'm going to WNEW. Is anyone expecting you?—Yes. The guy running the elevator, Jose, has the inside number, so he calls and says 'Your guests are here.' I put on the longest record I could find: Chicago's 'Ballet for a Girl in Buchannon.' It runs about 16 minutes. I hope the record doesn't skip, and [I] walk down the hall, get in the freight elevator, and go downstairs and there's John, May, and Richard. We ride up to the second floor. And what you hear is literally unfolding almost instantly once we get set up and I make sure Joe the engineer has tape running."

Dennis's cool demeanor masked the thoughts running around in his head.

"It's John Lennon. It's the biggest of all. It's someone literally 10 years prior I'm sitting in my home in Queens—I'm still a kid in school— and I'm taping him off *The Ed Sullivan Show*; that's reel-to-reel audio tape. It was very primitive, but you could do it. I was a teenager—I still have those tapes."

As a professional, Dennis knew that John was not there to tell him his favorite Beatles stories. He had come to promote his new album, *Walls and Bridges*. Dennis knew better than to start the interview off asking if The Beatles were ever going to get back together. That was the question on everyone's lips in those days. For the first 25 minutes they talk about John's new album. Off air, they converse about what they'll play next. Remember, this is all live as it happens, no rehearsal, no pre-production. Then came the moment off air in an offhand comment when John references a Beatles song, "Day Tripper." When he mentions the song, Dennis pulls the album out of the wall behind him.

"At WNEW the entire library was right behind you." Literally, it was free-form. "Day Tripper" was on *"Yesterday and Today,"* which is the famous butcher cover album. "It's the American version of the album, and I cued the song up and asked him off air about the butcher cover, and he starts to tell me the story, and I go 'hold it' because I knew we would be live in 30 seconds. I said, 'Save it for the air,' and he tells the story."

At that point John opened the door to telling Beatles stories. But Dennis tread lightly and didn't immediately rush in and turn the interview around to being a Beatles interview. About an hour in Dennis dipped a toe into the water and said, "'Can we talk about ...' and John interrupts me, and he says, 'Yeah, I know, I know,' and I said, 'Well, any plans.' And then he says, 'Are they getting back together?' Then he talks about why they would or wouldn't get together."

Another happy surprise of the day was that John brought a stack of his own 45s of oldies that he loved, played them on the air, and talked about how The Beatles picked certain riffs out of those songs. Before the interview when May Pang called to arrange it, she asked Dennis if John could bring some of his own records. Dennis thought he would bring albums that he's made or something to that effect, but he brought several 45s from his own collection.

"I didn't know at that time how important these seemingly obscure oldies were to him. He talks about 'listen to how this riff comes from this riff and influenced this song,' whether it's a Beatle, solo Lennon, or current song. This is all new to me and most of my listeners. It's happening on the air live for the first time. These days you would pretape, and you would cut things in and you would cut things out. This is live radio, so I'm doing this all on the fly. If I talk to John about something and think that I want to go to this record afterwards, I have to be prepared enough to have pulled that record out ahead of time and cue it up."

As their time together was drawing to a close, Dennis made sure to talk to John about his ongoing immigration struggles and his recent work producing an album for Harry Nilsson.

Dennis asked John if it made sense to him to be so important to so many people, to have been a member of a group that changed hairstyles and clothing. He asked if that made sense to John and if he could deal

121

with it. "John says, 'Well, I have to deal with it because I was in it. When I look back on it, its sort of vaguely astounding. The fact that I was there. But when you're in it…. We always called it the eye of the hurricane. It was calmer right in the middle than on the peripheral. We were part of whatever the '60s was, and we were the ones that were chosen to represent what was going on in the street. It was happening. It could have been somebody else, but it wasn't. It was us and the Stones and people like that. And here we are. And we went through it together." Trying to put it all in perspective, Dennis wonders if John can appreciate just how wonderful this experience has been for him, the fan, now DJ, interviewing one of his rock-and-roll heroes. "Without missing a beat, John compares it to his own experience just two years earlier meeting and playing with one of his heroes, Chuck Berry, for the first time."

The final song of the afternoon appropriately enough was "I Am the Walrus," chosen by John. Dennis remembers that "as the record is coming to an end, John asks me off air if I know what the mumbling dialogue is that you hear as the song fades. I tell John hold it 'for the air.' And so, for the first time on the air John explains how they just tuned into a live presentation of King Lear on the BBC and mixed it in."

The show couldn't have been better and has received many accolades over the years. Peter Asher called it the best John Lennon interview ever done. You can hear the entire interview on the John Lennon website and Dennis's website. www.denniselsas.com, where his archives also contain great highlights from his conversations with Elton John, Pete Townshend, Jerry Garcia, and more. The John Lennon interview is also part of the permanent collection at the Paley Center for Media in New York. Interview highlights are included in *The Beatles Anthology*, Ron Howard's documentary *Eight Days a Week*, the PBS film *Lennon NYC*, and numerous Beatles books and documentaries.

Looking back, Dennis says it's still his most memorable on-air experience and how warm, friendly, and funny John was that afternoon.

While John's interview was the longest and the most well known, he is not the only Beatle Dennis has come in contact with. In 1976 he was invited backstage at Madison Square Garden to chat with Paul and Linda McCartney when the Wings Over America tour came to New York City.

The local TV stations and the press had been teasing headlines all day: "Are the Beatles getting back together? Will John show up at the Garden?"

"There were always rumors going around," Dennis said. "There was really no way to predict what might happen."

When Dennis had his 15 minutes with Paul and Linda, among all the other journalists eagerly awaiting their spot, Dennis hinted at the question. Paul jokingly replied with this couplet: "The Beatles split in '69, and since then they've been doing fine. And if that question doesn't cease, ain't no one gonna get no peace." And he qualified that with a polite "probably not now, but you never know."

In those days Wings didn't play many Beatles songs. This was Paul's new band, and he was stretching those proverbial wings. Dennis asked Paul if at times it felt like the early days being back on tour, and Paul said that indeed it did.

"He was warm and charming," Dennis said. "Up close he still looked very much like the 'cute' Beatles. Together with Linda they were quite approachable, making it easy to talk with them."

Dennis got back to the station and used the music he had available to re-create the concert for a special to run on the air the next night. His opening line was "At long last there was long hair at Madison Square," quoting a line from their recent album *Venus and Mars* and the song "Rock Show."

And since 2006 Dennis has interviewed both Ringo and John's older son Julian Lennon, each separately on three different occasions.

There was the story of another memorable guest star at another concert that Dennis was happy to tell. He was live on air with Elton John in the days after that famous Thanksgiving concert where John Lennon appeared onstage and the two performed John's only number one hit as a solo artist, "Whatever Gets You Thru the Night." Elton played and sang on that record and bet John that if it hit number one, he would have to come onstage with him. John lost the bet. The two also sang The Beatles' classics, "Lucy in the Sky with Diamonds," which Elton had famously covered, and Paul's song "I Saw Her Standing There." The concert in 1974 turned out to be John Lennon's last time onstage before he was murdered in 1980.

Dennis welcomed Elton John into the studio the day after the concert, which was just two months after he had interviewed John Lennon. Elton told stories from that famous night for the first time on Dennis's show. With limited coverage on TV and in the press, the only place to hear the full story was on Dennis's radio show.

Sadly, just six years later the shot rang out. Like many people I spoke to, the night John Lennon was murdered is etched in Dennis's memory. On December 8, 1980, WNEW was hosting its annual Christmas Concert charity fundraiser. Nearly everyone from the station was at Avery Fischer Hall (now David Geffen Hall) at Lincoln Center.

"It's 11:00, the concert's over and there is a private gathering back-stage to celebrate the evening." Dennis recalls, "Someone reaches Scott Muni (program director) [by] phone. The word had gotten to the radio station and newsroom, first that John had been shot, then that he is dead. Scott shares the horrible news with the crowd, and of course the party is over. Without conferring with each other, individually all the DJs go back to the station. It became an all-night vigil live on the radio as listeners and DJs shared their sorrow and their memories. It was the only place I wanted to be."

Dennis went home that night and got his tape of the Lennon interview to get ready to air on his next shift at 6:00 the next night.

At this point let's roll back the clock and look at how Dennis got his start in radio. You could say it was all due to The Beatles invading America.

Becoming a DJ was only a fantasy in Dennis's head when he was growing up in Queens in the '60s. He loved rock and roll and the radio and listening to the great DJs on New York's top 40 stations WINS, WMCA, and WABC. Without Dennis realizing it at the time, all those voices were making an impression on him and no doubt played a part in influencing what would become his own unique style.

"I can't tell you exactly when I first heard a Beatles record, but I can remember that by late December 1963 all the top 40 stations in New York (and probably across the country) were battling to be 'The Beatles Station' in your town. I do remember making it a point to watch their first US TV appearance in early January on the Jack Paar show. And of course, their first and all the following Ed Sullivan appearances were must-see TV."

Dennis's passion for The Beatles intensified that love of radio and the DJs that brought him the music and information about his new favorite band.

"The radio was the primary way we heard and learned about The Beatles. There really was very little rock-and-roll press in those days. It was pre–*Rolling Stone* and preinternet, so there was no YouTube, Facebook, Twitter, Tick Tok, etc. The place to go to get your info and hear the music was the radio. You chose your favorite station, chose your favorite disc jockey, and listen[ed] to it evolve."

Times were changing when Dennis got to college in the mid–'60s. He started off as a political science major at Queens College. When he found out there was a speech department, he chose to pursue a double major of political science and speech. By the time he graduated he was a communications arts major, a new term being used for his course of study. It was in college that he got his first gig as a DJ on WQMC, the school radio station that he helped start. When he auditioned, there was no doubt that he had a knack and a talent for the job.

And as The Beatles were going from "Yeah, Yeah, Yeah" to "A Day in the Life" in only three years (1964–1967), rock radio was expanding from top 40 AM to include the new "progressive underground" format of FM and provide new opportunities for young DJs.

Beginning with a weekend FM show on a local (New Rochelle, New York) radio station in 1969, Dennis honed his craft and style and joined WNEW-FM, New York's premiere rock-and-roll station, on July 11, 1971. More than 50 years later, he is among America's most respected, recognizable, and influential rock-and-roll personalities. He is the "Voice of Rock History" at the Woodstock Museum at Bethel Woods Center for the Arts. Until the pandemic he toured with his multimedia show "Rock & Roll Never Forgets," and he hopes to bring it back to the public in the near future. He remains passionate about the lads from Liverpool and every week closes his Sirius/XM Fab Fourum show with the catchphrase "Beatles Forever."

In Dennis's life as well as ours it is indeed Beatles Forever.

Baby You Can Drive His ... Old, Rickety Jeep

The moment Darren DeVivo—well-known DJ and Beatles aficionado on WFUV, a popular public progressive radio station in New York City— met Paul McCartney could have been a sketch on *Saturday Night Live*. The year was about 1988, and Darren was 23, sitting in the back of his dad's rickety jeep with his mom in the passenger seat on their way out to Montauk Point from their vacation home in East Hampton. It's a trip the trio from the Bronx took hundreds of times over the years since Darren's dad bought the small house to keep up with his fishing obsession. The jeep was old and rusty from sitting on the sand in the salt air. For Darren, an only child, the excursion was like being "dragged to purgatory."

Darren was a Beatles fan from the time he was a toddler. He knew that the McCartneys had a home in East Hampton and always dreamed of what he would do if he ever saw that face! The local papers ran stories of McCartney sightings. The actual event was way beyond compare.

Ringo with Emily and her dad, WFUV DJ Darren DeVivo, at the NYCB Theater at Westbury in New York, 2010.

"Dad would take all the side roads to avoid the slowdowns on Montauk Highway, the one two-lane highway that cuts through all the villages. We're in Amagansett, the town between East Hampton and Montauk Point; we're coming out of one of the side streets approaching Montauk Highway, where he's going to get on the highway, and then it's a straight shot out to Montauk. So, I'm sitting in the back seat of the car, [and] I see a car go by in front of us—I do see a woman with blonde hair in the car, she caught my eye, but I didn't think anything of it. My mother, whose sitting in the front seat passenger side, said, 'You know, the woman in the car looked like Linda.' I thought *Did it really? It wasn't, I'm sure.* We're in Amagansett; it's only a couple of miles, but I didn't think of the McCartneys being settled in Amagansett. I knew that there was a residence the Eastman's [Linda's family] owned in East Hampton. So, I'm not thinking that they're driving around the side roads in Amagansett. Within seconds as my dad pulled into the intersection to make the left onto Montauk Highway, I see a guy on a bicycle and kids around him on bikes. I'm not really paying close attention—this all happened so fast. Next thing I knew my mother says, 'I don't believe it! I think that's Paul McCartney across the street!' By the time he was crossing Montauk Highway cars were beeping at him, waving, and slowing down. He

126

had been recognized. He was waving back, and he was coming right for us. It's Montauk Highway—it's just a busy two-lane main street. So, he's coming across towards us, and then I spot him. *It's him!! It's him!! Oh, my goodness!* I think my first reaction was to try to get out of the car. The problem is a lot of the chassis was rusted. So, the back doors—the door I was sitting at.... I couldn't open the door! It was rusted shut! Which means I had probably been getting in the car on the other side. I didn't believe it. Here's Paul McCartney! My mother goes flying out of the car to get his attention. I can't get out of the car! ... I'm putting my shoulder into the door—can't get it open. Finally I roll the window down, reach my arm out, and pop the car from the outside. I was able to open it from the outside! And that's how I got out, by putting my arm around and out the window! Meanwhile, my dad's scrambling because he has a legal pad—why?—I don't know but he has a legal pad in the jeep. He quick grabbed the legal pad and gives it to me. I manage to finally get out of the car, and all I remember is that my mother was talking to Paul. My dad was yelling out to him [imitating his father's gravelly voice with a Bronx accent 'Hey Paul, he's your biggest fan—he's got your records all over the house.' It was very comical. I think Paul found it humorous or he thought 'Who are these freaks?' I don't remember what I said to him. It had to be something like 'You don't understand. I've been a fan since I was four years old.' He scribbled his name on the legal pad. I remember him saying 'You have very nice parents.' The kids were with him. One of them was James, his son, and it must have been friends. They didn't stop—they crossed the highway. I guess they knew where they were going—it was a family-type area of Amagansett where they were staying ... [and] he was like 'I got to go—I can't stop. The boys kept going.' And he said goodbye and was up on his bike and kept going. The whole thing happened in like a minute.

As we're driving away, I'm on cloud nine. But I'm also like 'What just happened?' You wouldn't think this was a celebrity because he physically looked like he slept in his car. He had big, baggy, ratty shorts, a white T-shirt ... [and] his hair was kind of messy—it wasn't really combed. He very much looked like the local that you wouldn't pay any attention to."

Darren later found out the McCartney's were renting a farm or a big house and that Paul was rehearsing for the upcoming 1989 world tour. He also could have been working on songs for the *Flowers in the Dirt* album.

That's the closest Darren, in his lengthy career in radio, has every gotten to Paul McCartney. But being a DJ has put him in an enviable position. Darren has met Ringo three times and more Beatles icons, albeit in a more structured way. Darren has also had the pleasure of interviewing Beatles' children—James (Paul's son, all grown up sans bicycle), Dhani Harrison (George's lookalike son), Julian Lennon (John's son from his first marriage to Cynthia), members of the Quarrymen (John and Paul's first band), and Geoff Emerick, The Beatles' engineer.

Wait, what?! Ringo! Let's talk about Ringo!

First there was the quick meet-and-greet where about five couples from the radio station won VIP tickets and backstage passes to a concert on Long Island. As the DJ representing the station, Darren brought them back, got the chance to shake Ringo's hand, and doesn't even remember what he said.

Then came the day Darren will never forget. In 2003 he sat down with Ringo for a 20-minute interview. *Ringo Rama* had just come out, and Ringo's publicist contacted the station to give Ringo the chance to promote it. Darren pushed and shoved to make sure he was the one to get the chance to properly interview one of his idols.

It was like a scene out of *Notting Hill*. The interview was set at a suite in the Carlisle Hotel in Manhattan. Darren and his engineer Chris, who was taking care of the mics and the recording equipment, stood in front of the hotel suite door. Once inside Darren, with butterflies in his stomach, was able to be professional and stay focused. He told Chris to keep an eye on the equipment and not to ask Darren any questions—from the time Darren sat down it was like he had blinders on.

"Next thing you know the door opens and in flies this little guy! And he was very cool! Very hyper and hyped up to do an interview. Twenty minutes, that's it—not a minute more boys. And we had a good 20-minute conversation."

Being the professional Darren is, he knew Ringo was there to push his new album and probably didn't want to spend 20 minutes bombarded with Beatles questions. So, that's exactly what they did. The interview was all about *Ringo Rama*.

There was a special personal moment Darren and Ringo shared. At that time Darren's daughter Emily was just four years old. She was in a body cast for six weeks due to major hip surgery she needed to treat a rare infection in her hip bone. She couldn't move for six weeks. Just like her dad, she liked Ringo even at age four. "We would watch *Yellow Submarine* together. Kids pick up on Ringo," Darren said. Emily knew that her dad would be meeting Ringo, so she drew him a picture. Darren brought it with him. Before the interview he gave Ringo the picture and told him what she was going through.

"When the interview was over, I broke out a copy of the *Good Night Vienna* album, and he signed it!" He also signed a CD booklet of *Ringo Rama* for Emily. But when Chris the engineer pulled out his dad's *White Album*, Ringo would not autograph it. He said, "'I only gave it to the little girl because she's sick and she gave me the picture. All right boys—thank you—gotta go shopping.' And he's out the door like a comet. And, it was like, he's good.... He had this internal clock that knew 20 minutes is up and now it's my time—I'm outta here."

Ringo was everything Darren hoped he would be ... but maybe just a touch smaller.

"You know he's small, but when you're with him you're like Damn! You're small. He's a little guy. But he was definitely a burst of energy. He didn't walk; he seemed to bounce."

About seven years later, Emily got the chance to meet Ringo with her dad. It was another concert on Long Island this time with Ringo Starr & His All-Starr Band. Ringo's publicist gave Darren and Emily the all clear to go backstage and say hi. The show was about to start, so it was a quick meeting and Ringo took a cool picture with the two of them. Darren didn't get the chance to explain that this was the little girl of the picture fame—all grown up. But one of the thrills of that night was when Darren and Emily were sitting in the front row. Midshow, Ringo reached down and took a handful of popcorn from Emily's bucket!

What made Darren obsess over The Beatles and especially Paul for a lifetime? He jokingly blames whoever does this in the netherworld. "They put in me ... Beatles' Fan, McCartney Fan, Mets Fan, from day one." His parents, not big fans themselves, played along. Every Christmas he got a Beatles record beautifully wrapped. Until this day, when Christmas rolls around he goes into a Beatles mode. "I don't know what drew me to The Beatles or to music. Something that intrigued me. Whether it was a photo on an album cover or whether it was having an Apple record and an Apple spinning on my little Show 'N' Tell phonograph I don't know."

Growing up in the '70s Darren followed their solo careers, especially Wings, and learned about The Beatles through that. There weren't many books in those early years after the breakup. He would buy the occasional magazine that would pop up in the local candy store. He did have two books, *The Beatles Forever* by Nicolas Shaffner and the book he calls his Beatles bible, *Growing Up with the Beatles* by Ron Schaumburg.

The picture-laden book documents the author's adolescence in relation to Beatles music being released. He regales the reader with stories of going on his first date, the prom, his first job with new Beatles music as his soundtrack, and then the breakup and the craziness with Yoko.

"It's an interesting book in that regard," Darren said. He read it and thumbed through it hundreds of times. Recently Darren had a full-circle moment with his adolescent favorite book. As he was scrolling through eBay for more Beatles memorabilia, he stumbled across items listed as items from Ron Schaumberg's youth. "So, I did a little research, and it turns out he's still alive, but he's in pharmaceuticals or something like that. It seems as though late in age his days as a Beatles fan served their purpose, and he's selling off everything that he got when he was young that he used in his book that I grew up reading. His book was like one of my bibles! So, I bought a few singles! I thought it was a strange turn of events that a book that I thumbed through all the time in the late '70s [and] early '80s, [and] now I own a couple of records that were probably photographed and are in the book."

Darren has shaped his life around his music passion, which started with The Beatles. "Music has always been front and center in my life." The Beatles were front and center in the music world, and nothing faded. "My interests remained. Even when I wasn't necessarily thrilled with some of the solo stuff he [Paul McCartney] was doing, I was hardcore. I never waivered as a fan of the whole thing. When I got older and hit my 20s I decided to get into the heavy lifting. Get all the Lennon albums, all the Ringo albums [he already had lots of George's albums], more books, more reading; it was cementing itself to the point where— here I am—I'm 56, I'm cohosting a Beatles podcast [*Things We Said Today* on Apple Podcasts]. I've got Beatles collectibles, more so music related, records, CDs, books, all over the place," Darren said.

"The Beatles strengthened my love for music at an early age." That passion led Darren to a lifelong career as a popular DJ in the city that John Lennon loved so much and in one of the world's largest radio markets in the country—New York.

Tom Frangione

Tom Frangione is a popular Beatles Channel DJ who hosts
a rarities show called *Way Beyond Compare* and is a cohost
of the channel's *Apple Jam* and *Fab Fourum* programs.

Five. The DJs Who Keep the Records Spinning

Did you ever wonder where Beatles Channel DJ Tom Frangione gets the rarities he plays on his show *Way Beyond Compare*? Well, a good many of them come directly from his private collection that has taken nearly 50 years to accumulate. If you hear a rare English B-side that was only on the CD single, there's a solid chance it came from his extensive collection. And he hasn't stopped working on it.

"I don't collect a lot of lunch boxes and things like that," Tom said. "I collect audio performances. So, whether it's radio broadcasts or import-only tracks or download-only tracks or anything like that, that's what does it for me."

In fact, just moments before he picked up the phone for our interview, he was compiling the non–CD releases that are surrounding the new *Get Back* project.

"There was the audio stream that they released through the streaming services of the full rooftop show," he said. "And there was this little glitch that happened with our *Let It Be* box sets. They didn't really give you the exact, correct, 1969 Glyn Johns *Get Back* album mix. The only

Ringo and Beatles Channel DJ Tom Frangione, 2014.

131

place it showed up, just by some weird, freaky, manufacturing glitch, is in Japan. So, you had to get the Japanese one to get the official 1969 mix." It's digging deep and finding gems such as this that "float his boat."

When the executives at the Beatles Channel tossed around the idea of doing a rarities show, they knew Tom was their go-to guy. Since Sirius XM works in direct partnership with Apple Corps, it doesn't have a hard time getting copies of the core catalog albums we all love such as *Please, Please Me, Let It Be, Sgt. Pepper,* and so on.

"But the solo stuff, particularly because it runs very broad, was something that they knew I could not only provide and have access to but could speak to and say, 'This was a bonus cut on the "Figure of Eight" CD single that only came out in England'—or whatever colors that in."

But Tom, while outstanding on all his Beatles Channel shows, is not a career radio guy. This makes his work at the station and his gig writing for *Beatlefan Magazine* somewhat labors of love. The "cape he wears" Monday through Friday is that of chief financial officer for a 50-physician medical group. As he contemplates hanging up that cape, he is looking forward to perhaps doing more on the Beatles Channel.

With only limited radio experience, Tom was asked to audition for all three shows he appears on. And he hoped he passed the audition! In addition to *Way Beyond Compare,* Tom is the cohost of *Apple Jam* and the guy they call "the resident Beatles expert" on *Fab Fourum,* hosted by Dennis Elsas and Bill Flanagan.

"I was thrilled to death and honored to be asked to audition for all three of the shows. I'm glad that Sirius was able to find a home and find that right niche for someone who wasn't a career radio guy. I've done some fill-in radio over the years but was happy that there was a home for somebody on this very boutique—and high-profile—channel who could be the resident go-to guy and even an archive resource."

The first show Tom was asked to audition for was *Fab Fourum.* They had Dennis Elsas, a great veteran radio voice—in the business for over 50 years—and well known from his days on New York's ground-breaking FM radio station WNEW. They also lined up a seasoned and well-respected journalist and interviewer, Bill Flanagan.

"What they wanted to add to the mix was someone who had knowledge of The Beatles' music as a group and their solo work that was both broad and deep and who was a passionate fan as well,"

After success with the *Fab Fourum,* the powers that be landed on the idea of a rarities show. There was no doubt Tom was the guy to do it. But logistically what would it look like? Would it be an hour a week, a half hour a week, or once a month? "It's still radio, and you can't be playing all off-the-wall stuff for hours at a time," Tom said. "The general fan or just someone tuning in is thinking *I thought this was* the *Beatles Channel. Why am I listening to Billy Preston doing 'Will It Go Round in Circles'?* Unless they know that this is with Ringo and the All-Starr Band and that is why we put it on the show." The show is now half an hour long with a new episode running four times a week.

Fans and collectors eat this stuff up, as shown by the emails Tom gets for the show.

They say things like "it's cool that you guys mix it up and we get to hear things besides 'Nowhere Man' and 'Please, Please, Me' for a half hour at a time. And by the way, where did you get that download track? I never heard of it?" Other collectors say "Yeah, I think I have a decent collection but even I never heard that one." What Tom loves most is when people ask where they can get their hands on an obscure track and he is able to lead them to the Promised Land. On the morning of our interview, he answered someone who wrote in and said, "I heard a version of 'Hey Bulldog' that ends cold, and they're talking in the studio and John says 'All right! Quiet!' I've looked high and low on the internet, and I can't find it. It's not a bootleg. I'm coming to you because if anyone knows this answer it's you."

Tom jokes that flattery will get you everywhere, but there's nothing like putting a guy on the spot. "If I can't come up with this, I will disappoint somebody. But fortunately, I knew where that one came from. I told the guy that was one of those Rock Band video game mixes that has the Fab Four chatter on the front and the end of it to give it a feel of being in the studio." The listener wrote back a gushing thank-you email, saying he couldn't thank him enough and that he was now able to find it. While Tom won't reveal his own sources for the truly rare (and in some cases unreleased) material, he loves giving people the leads they need to do their own hunting. He does this not only for his own show he also helps when folks send emails to other shows and others might be stumped.

The idea for *Apple Jam* actually came from executives at Apple. The idea was to spotlight other Apple artists in their catalog. These include great musicians who are woven into today's culture in their own way such as Badfinger, James Taylor, Billy Preston, and Mary Hopkin. "It was a very interesting proposition," Tom said. "But the potential limitation is that there are about 30 albums' worth of music. Five of those albums are Yoko Ono albums, 2 of them are Ravi Shankar, and 2 are by John Tavener. That wouldn't be what the channel was going to sound like for a half hour or an hour at a time. We've played tracks from all three of those artists. We've played Ravi Shankar, we've played Yoko One more than once, and we've played John Tavener. But it's not the kind of thing you can continuously go back to."

That said, the amount of music that comprises the 30 or so albums gets whittled down pretty quickly, and simply playing cuts from albums would not sustain a show.

Tom and his cohost David Fricke broaden the scope of the playlist by including music from the box set *Good as Gold* with music published by Apple or even recorded at Apple Studios.

With Apple's permission, Tom and David also play recordings that were never released. You may have heard the Frank Sinatra acetate disc or the Badfinger (Iveys) Christmas record on the show. And that is the only place you would have the opportunity to hear them. Since the music mix is so eclectic, it was decided that the show would run for one hour, with a new episode once a month played four times a week.

"That's what you would have to call a very boutique show," Tom said. "The reaction we get to *Apple Jam* shows up in the emails. People are very, very passionate. They say things like 'Thank God somebody is finally shedding a light on Pete Ham [lead vocalist and composer with Badfinger] as a songwriter and Badfinger. They should be in the Hall of Fame.' They are very passionate about it."

Being a Beatles Channel DJ comes with drool-worthy perks. Tom has met Paul and Ringo more than once, but the time he met them both on the same night at Abbey Road Studios was an event that walked straight out of his dreams. It was the 50th anniversary party in 2019 to celebrate the release of *Abbey Road*. There was a big party to celebrate the anniversary and the release of the box set that was coming out. Tom was invited, and even before he heard Paul and Ringo would be there, he knew he had to go. He couldn't pass up the chance to hear the album on what could be called the best sound system in the world in the place where it was recorded, and then the studio was named after the album. It being his all-time favorite album, he jokes that "the rule in my hometown of Scotch Plains, NJ is that if Tom is listening to *Abbey Road*, so are his neighbors."

Tom said, "Yeah, sure I'll go to that party! And as the event neared it became the world's worst-kept secret that both Paul and Ringo would show up and join the celebration. I got to meet both of them—as well as Olivia Harrison and Giles Martin—on the same night. That was a thrill."

Tom has had the pleasure of meeting both Paul and Ringo individually several times. He said both are so genuine and disarming that they take you right to a place of normal conversation.

"Certainly, with Ringo it's never a dull moment. Even when it's a quick hello before a concert he'll say something that'll just take me so far off my game. I want to rehearse in my head saying 'Oh, Ringo. Good to see you again. I'm Tom from the Beatles Channel, and it's an honor to be here.' And he'll say something so disarming that you get right into a normal conversation. When I was introduced to him at one of the events and I launched into 'I'm Tom from the Beatles Channel ...' and he looked me right in the eye and said, 'The Beatles Channel is the best decision we ever made.' At that point what are you supposed to say beyond 'Thank you,' or 'Are you sure?' But at that point they have you disarmed, and you're ready to go into conversation mode. Because you know how many people say 'I'm your biggest fan. I have all your records, and your music has made a profound influence on my life.' Do you know how many people tell him that? Everybody! I'm sure they never get tired of hearing that. I know I wouldn't. But I think they want to have more of a conversation. Paul is the king of that. When I saw him at the Abbey Road event..."

At this point Tom makes a point that it's harder to get to meet Paul than Ringo, and he's only met Paul three or four times in his entire life! Three or four times!! I'm still going for that one thrilling moment when I lean in for a Paul hug. Back to Tom.

"When I saw him at the Abbey Road event ...—you reintroduce yourself to him—I say 'I'm Tom from the Beatles Channel. I do the *Fab Fourum*.' And he knocks you right down and he says 'Oh, the *Fab Fourum*. I listen to you all the time on the radio.' It's like no, shut up! My next sentence was 'I've been listening to *you* on the radio.' They get you right into a conversation. It says something about how many times they must have had to do this over the years. As you can imagine, it's a thrill to be part of a conversation like that!"

Tom had the chance to be with Ringo one-on-one for nearly an hour when he interviewed him in honor of the 40th anniversary of his album *Stop and Smell the Roses*.

"I always thought it was a terrific record and very overlooked, but more importantly it happened at a very crucial time in his life and his career. It was also the anniversary of meeting Barbara to whom he's been married for that full 40 years. Both Paul and George are on the album, and John was to have been on the album. They had met as late as Thanksgiving time in 1980. You may have heard some of the demos and things where John has said 'Oh, this is a good one. I'll give it to Ringo.' There were songs that John had written, and they were planning to record in January of 1981. Between the two Beatles showing up, the timing of John, the timing of Barbara and how music changed that very year with a little thing called MTV where now there was a visual component—that had to be addressed too. There were so many things going on at that time, and we thought it would be a good time to revisit the album and give it a new life."

Tom knew the last thing Ringo wanted to talk about at this point was his time with The Beatles and so didn't bring that up. Ringo enjoyed the interview so much that when the allotted time was coming to an end, his manager motioned to Tom to keep it going. The Beatles Channel also added songs from *Stop and Smell the Roses* back into rotation.

Paul also agreed to a tremendous hour-long interview on the Beatles Channel to celebrate the 50th anniversary of *Ram*, the only album that's credited to Paul and Linda and that means a lot to him. Hosted by Lou Simon, the special that included the interview and music from the album was lauded by the channel's listeners.

Paul and Ringo are extremely supportive of the Beatles Channel. As a matter of fact, everything related to The Beatles is done under the auspices of Apple. It is the vehicle by which *Get Back* (the docuseries) got done. Apple has final approval on all matters tied to The Beatles' ongoing legacy—whether it be an official radio channel, a new line of T-shirts or lunch boxes, and of course any type of music or film release such as the *Let It Be* box set and the *Beatles 1* DVD or, most recently, the *Get Back* series. Yoko Ono Lennon, Olivia Harrison, Paul, and Ringo are still the four official voices and are happy to work closely with the Beatles Channel.

"So, for example, if we say okay, Ringo, you have a new album out; can [we] get liners for each of the 12 songs? More often than not they oblige, and we end up with something like 'Hi this is Ringo—this is a song from my new album *What's My Name*, and the song is called 'Grow Old with Me,' written by John Lennon. And here it is on the Beatles Channel," Tom said.

"Anytime we need support from them they're quick to respond and usually affirmative. Apple is our green light for whatever we want to do."

If you are a Beatles Channel fan, you know that the channel often plays the music that inspired The Beatles. At any given time, you could hear Carl Perkins or Elvis or Little Richard. A casual listener may not understand why that music is played on something called the Beatles Channel. But the answer is simple.

"It's not just a channel *of* The Beatles—it's a channel *for* The Beatles," Tom explained. "Paul and Ringo and the team at Apple are very involved in this. They are very passionate about it, and these are the records that maybe Paul and Ringo want to hear. It's *for* them as well as *about* them. And the funny part is you can hear how The Beatles incorporated that stuff into their own music."

Toms says that he is "thrilled and honored to be a part of The Beatles Channel."

Breakfast with the Beatles: Ken Dashow

These shows happen all over the country. This particular one is aired on Q104.3 in New York.

"What did The Beatles, the biggest explosion in the world, what did The Beatles do? The Beatles fired The Beatles— the mop tops. They took off the suits and stopped touring. The number one touring band in the world stopped touring," Ken Dashow, host of *Breakfast with The Beatles*, said, still sounding astonished. Of course, when the touring stopped, they recorded the iconic album *Sgt. Pepper*, which changed the landscape of pop music forever.

"Most musicians find the thing they do and do

Ken Dashow, host of *Breakfast with The Beatles* on Q104.3 in New York, 2018.

it until they're not successful anymore. Not the Beatles," Ken said. "No band has the breadth and width of output in the seven years they recorded that The Beatles had. They wrote children's songs. They wrote complex psychedelic jams for hipsters and hippies. They wrote intimate emotional songs, angry songs, happy and political songs."

That's why *Breakfast with the Beatles* is still popular, Ken said.

Forty percent of our audience are children and teenagers. Five-year-olds and 70-year-olds have the same joy on their faces when the music comes on. I defy any other act to pull that together. There's something technical and spiritual about their music. What's magic about The Beatles is one word: love. "All You Need Is Love," "Say the word, love," "She Loves You," Love, love, love. That message will never be old. It was needed in 1964, and it's needed more now.

Lots of people tell me the first song their children or grandchildren learned to sing is "Yellow Submarine." It [the music] is a multigenerational thing that everyone shares. A grandfather might not play Fortnite [a popular video game] with his grandchildren, but they can listen to *Breakfast with the Beatles* and all enjoy it.

Ken Dashow has been hosting the popular *Breakfast with the Beatles* radio show since 2004. It started quite simply. It was the 40th anniversary of The Beatles coming to America, and Ken thought he would play some Beatles music. His program manager told him to play all Beatles music. Ken was known around the station as the Beatles expert, so he was able to throw in interesting factoids between songs. He recalled that

One day [after that], I came in to do an afternoon show, and [my program manager] had a weird grin on his face. He said, "We've never gotten a response like that to anything we've ever done on this station."

I said, "Wow! Maybe next year we'll do it again."

He said, "Why not next week?" Then he said, "This Beatles thing, I think we'll keep doing it."

I said, "For how long?"

He said, "Until I tell you to stop."

Well, he's moved on to LA and San Diego, and it's [2022], and no one's ever told me to stop.

In the last 18 years, Ken has interviewed all sorts of musical giants who were the band's contemporaries or were influenced by and loved The Beatles. These include Graham Nash (Crosby, Stills, and Nash), who was in the Hollies at the time of The Beatles, and Don McLean (singer-songwriter of "American Pie" fame). Don McLean told Ken during an interview that The Beatles taught him that every word counts. He said he used to write poetry and sing it, but The Beatles taught him that there isn't one word that's wasted. "That hit me right between the eyes," Ken said.

Ken's most memorable interviews were with the boys themselves. He had the good fortune to interview both Paul McCartney and Ringo Starr.

> Paul carries the weight of fame easier and more effortlessly. There are people with one record that have loads of security guards. I saw Paul coming out of Central Park one day after a jog. He had a Poland Springs bottle. I said, "Hi Paul," and he said, "Oh, hey," and kept on walking. Here's one of the biggest stars, he said, "You try to put good karma in the world and hope it comes back." He is one of the greatest singers and songwriters of the 20th century and beyond. I put him on the shelf with Beethoven, Mozart, and Gershwin.

When asked if he was nervous when he interviewed the master himself, Ken sang the familiar song. "He gets it. He understands how nervous you are. He talks for a while while you calm down and settle a bit. You get to breathe and think and then get into a conversation."

Ringo is a little more reserved, Ken said.

> The first time I met Ringo, it was almost like he was being brought here for a jury [trial]. He answered questions. We didn't chat much. I told him I'm an amateur drummer and how hard it was for a right-hander to go around the kit like he does. He chuckled and said, "Well, that's your problem." After that, it was like we were old friends. He would say "Ah, there's Ken," and give me a big hug. That's because I wasn't obnoxious. I didn't ask stupid questions; I didn't bring anything for him to sign. It was like I passed an entrance exam.
>
> The next time I interviewed him he said "Tell me about radio," and we started chatting. It was like friends getting to know each other. He's been like that on phone calls and everything else. I understand the wall. He was in a pressure cooker; you have to be careful who you let through the gate.

Of course, I asked Ken which Beatle he identifies with the most.

"I read a thing once that said 'Which Beatles sign are you?' My wife tells me I'm most like Paul: happy, smiling, and you don't have to peel back layers to find me. She says I'm the outgoing one. I have to accept that!"

Ken has been asked who the bigger genius is, Paul or John:

> I say it's like two geniuses pulling on a rope. The rope is taught, and the greatest thing is the tension and magic in the rope. They complete each other and push each other.

Even though they couldn't read music, their ears were so attuned all the time. Paul and John listened to classical and atonal modern jazz. Those elements are in Beatles songs. There is so much complexity and twisting of notes that go into pop songs. Then there's the heartbreaking poetry.

That is why The Beatles are timeless.

Six

Paperback Writers and Collectors

"Dear Sir or Madam, Will you read my book? It took me years to write. Will you take a look?" I had no idea how true those words were until I started my endeavor on this book. It has been four wonderful years of finding like-minded folks and hearing wonderful stories, but it has also been a lot of hard work.

The following writers, all Beatle lovers, embarked on their journeys with excitement, dedication, and a hard work ethic. The results are mind-blowing. These are just a sample of the authors I had the opportunity to chat with. I hope you enjoy their stories as much as I did.

Let It All Shine On

The John Lennon Series

Did you ever wonder what John Lennon was wearing on the first day of a ski weekend with his first wife, Cynthia? Did you want to be a fly on the wall and see what they ate for dinner, hear what they talked about, and learn what room they stayed in that night?

Lots of books talk about The Beatles and events in their lives. But the John Lennon series, painstakingly written by Beatles expert Jude Southerland Kessler, may be the only books that answer these questions and more. When you pick up one of the books it reads like a novel, but every piece of dialogue and every detail, down to the socks on their feet, are factual. Every description, every movement, is documented; a recent release contained 4,600 footnotes. The facts are blended into a fascinating story. You are taken on a ride of dramatic twists and turns, great highs and great lows, all done with grace and humor.

For nearly 40 years, Jude has been burning the midnight oil

researching and writing her series eight days a week. A work in progress, the series will cover John Lennon's short life from his birth in 1940 through his tragic death in 1980. A recent release, volume four in the series, *Should Have Known Better*, covers The Beatles' heyday in 1964. It was originally meant to cover 1964–1965, but when Jude got to 900 pages and she was still on '64, she knew she had to split it up. When it's finished, her series will consist of 10 books.

Jude didn't have such lofty ambitions in mind when she started the project. Her husband was a naval officer, meaning they moved 32 times in 40 years, sometimes spending only three months in one place. She was never able to make close friends or grow any roots. To ward off loneliness and boredom, she had to think of something that would be both meaningful and portable.

Jude finished high school when she was just 17. She went on to finish college in three years with a double major in English and history, and she has a master's degree in English. The only logical answer was to write a book about someone she knew. The first person who came to mind was John Lennon, a man Jude has been obsessed with since 1963 when she was in fourth grade. Naively, she thought she knew everything about him. Within the first

week of starting research, she discovered she had a lot to learn. In her words, she knew "absolutely nothing" about John Lennon.

Jude leaves no stone unturned in her stories.

"The days when The Beatles were recording 'Love Me Do' in the studio, everyone knows from regular books that they went to eat lunch with George Martin [their producer] at the Alpino [restaurant]. I called the Alpino and asked if they could give me any pictures of the building from the early 1960s because I have to be able to describe it. Then I wrote to

Jude Southerland Kessler in her Beatles writing room, 2016.

142

Giles Martin [George's son] and said, 'I have some questions for your dad. They're very weird questions, but I'm trying to tell John's life story as a narrative. I need to know when they left EMI [Studios] to go to the Alpino. How did they get there? Did they go in a taxi? Did they walk? Did they take George's car? What kind of car was it? What did it look like? What did the interior look like, because I have to be able to describe it?' He answered and said they were the strangest questions anyone has ever asked. But it's details I have to know. So, it's a different sort of animal than a regular Beatles book."

Jude doesn't stop at asking people who were there. For every detail, she goes through her collection of 500 Beatles books looking for anything about that event. She marks them all and takes copious notes that could be up to 80 pages long. Then she goes back and checks off each fact.

The first book took 18 years to write. In that time, Jude and her husband went to Liverpool seven times and forged relationships with John's inner circle, including his best friend from college and The Beatles' first manager. That was the bulk of the research; now it's just going back and filling in the spaces, she said. Her husband has been her partner every step of the way. "He took notes while I did interviews," she said. He paid all the self-publishing costs. "We are partners in everything we do."

Jude chose to write her series as narrative nonfiction for people who didn't want to just read the facts. "I thought people might want to read a story about a boy who had never been loved, who decided that he would change the world through his music, and he would make people sorry that they didn't love him. He would prove to them that he was valuable and worthy. It's a great, great, sad story," Jude said.

Jude and her husband have one son and have fostered many children when their son was growing up. "We had kids that were abandoned or in other turmoil," she said. "They lived with us from six months to a year. We always had a child with us. But John 'lived' with us the longest. John grew up without love. Every song was about how lost and abandoned he was."

Jude took John's tragic death as if a family member had been murdered. That fateful day, her husband was set to come home from a nine-month deployment, a tour that was originally going to be six months but was delayed. "I had my dress laid out on the bed," she said. "The house was all clean, and I had fresh flowers. I was getting ready to leave when the phone rang. It was the CO's [commanding officer's] son. He told me he had some horrible news and that I'd better sit down.

I thought they'd been delayed again. Don't tell me they are going to be delayed again. I never expected him to say 'John Lennon's been shot.'"

When her husband came down the gangplank, he had tears in his eyes just as Jude did. They didn't have to say anything; they just knew.

As an eight-year-old child, Jude had felt drawn to John. He was a leader; he formed the band. He was the one in charge, and he was smart, but he wasn't her first choice. "In December 1963 I was in fourth grade," she said. "A friend walked up to me as soon as I got off the bus. She showed me a picture in a magazine and said, 'These are The Beatles. Everyone's in love with one. You have to pick one before recess.' Recess was at 10:00. I looked at the picture and said, 'George.' That night I learned more about the band. I found out John was the leader. He was the glue. When I went back to school the next day and told my friend I changed my pick to John, she said, 'That's who we knew you would pick.'"

Almost 50 years later, Jude's passion for John has grown exponentially. "I feel very driven to tell this story," she said. "I believe beyond a shadow of a doubt that's what I came here to do. That's my job. I'm supposed to get it done. I feel like I'm not doing the right thing if I don't work on it."

The first five books of Jude's John Lennon series have recently become accepted as part of the permanent collection of The Rock & Roll Hall of Fame's Library and Archives.

Songs They were Singing

Music journalist Kit O'Toole, EdD, author of *Songs We Were Singing: Guided Tours Through the Beatles' Lesser-Known Tracks* and *Michael Jackson FAQ: All That's Left to Know About the King of Pop*, says she owes her career to the Fab Four. She has been writing her entire life, but it was her off-the-charts excitement of seeing Paul McCartney in concert for the first time in 1989 that set her on her path to music journalism. "I was so excited just to be in the same vicinity as him. I kept saying to myself, 'This is a Beatle! This is Paul McCartney! He's right there!!' It was a big moment to see him live. He hadn't toured for so long. When he launched into his Beatles stuff, I said, 'I can't believe I'm watching the man who created this stuff!' It's a moment I'll never forget."

Kit was a senior in high school and editor of the student paper when the historic concert took place. She was a "tad excited" and couldn't help but write an emotional review of the concert given by the man himself. That's when she realized she could affect somebody through her writing.

"After the paper came out, I was walking to class. There was this teacher. He was a coach and taught health class; he wasn't 'Mr. Warmth,' and I never had that much to do with him. He stopped me and he said, 'I just want to tell you I read your article. You made me feel like a kid again. I remember what it was like to be a Beatles fan.' Then I knew I could really touch someone." Still, despite this early promising start, Kit's career path wasn't a straight line. "There weren't a lot of opportunities for music journalists in those days. You could try to get a job at *Rolling Stone*, but good luck with that." So, she went to grad school and got a PhD in instructional technology, but she knew all along that her heart wasn't in it. She took some time off before getting a job in academia.

"I started writing a blog just for fun about music," Kit said. "I got hired at Blogcritics. I wrote a ton of Beatles stuff, and that got me the *Michael Jackson FAQ* book. So it was the combo of technology and self-publishing that ended up with me publishing my first Beatles book." She is currently working on the sequel.

Kit realized that she could make a career out of her passion. Now she writes a column called "Hard Day's Night" for *Beatlefan* magazine and her own "Deep Beatles" column. She also runs a podcast called *Talk More Talk* about the lads.

Kit's passion has led her on many magical mystery journeys. She was a presenter at the GRAMMY Museum Mississippi in Cleveland, Mississippi, and she's a presenter at the Beatles at the Ridge Music Festival in Walnut Creek, Arkansas. If it were not for The Beatles, those two places would never have been on her radar. As it is, she has many friends from those trips, and let's not forget her trips to London and Liverpool.

Born in the early '70s, Kit was late to the party. Growing up she was surrounded by music, whether it was her dad playing guitar or listening to jazz and rock. Her father would play "Norwegian Wood," "Yesterday," and "Let it Be," but it wasn't until she was a bit older that she appreciated the music.

In the mid-'80s when she hit 13, Kit was dutifully listening to Wham and Duran Duran when one day in eighth-grade chorus class someone brought in The Beatles' *20 Greatest Hits* album for the class to hear. "I wasn't paying much attention," she said. "Then 'Eight Days a Week' came on. I'd never heard anything like that—the beat, the chord changes, the catchiness. It made me look up and say 'What's that? Maybe I've blown off this band.' I went to a local record store and bought the album on cassette. Then I bought all the albums [on vinyl] a bit at a time. Then I started getting into rarities and B-sides, singles, and documentaries."

None of Kit's friends were listening to The Beatles. Kit had to teach them about the band. When *Cloud 9* came out, she had to tell them who George Harrison was. It was hard to network with other fans. There was no internet. She subscribed to *Beatlefan* magazine in the '80s and started going to conventions in the early '90s. She found her people and has made great friendships through the music, but perhaps the best thing that happened through her love for the band was how it helped her bond with her parents—even in some unexpected ways.

In 1989, her mother stood in line for hours with Kit to buy tickets to the first Paul show because she didn't want her daughter to wait by herself at just age 17. Then, the next year Kit's mother saved the day! There was a concert to be held at Soldier Field in Chicago. When the tickets went on sale by phone, there were two numbers you could call. Kit told the story:

"Tickets went on sale when I was in school, so my mom made the call. I came home from school; she got the tickets; everything was fine. A couple of days later in the *Chicago Tribune* there was a small piece that said if you got tickets at this number, you're out of luck. The people on that line were not connected to the computer system. By the time they were, the tickets were sold out! To say the least, I was devastated. My mother was so mad that she looked up the address of Jam Productions and wrote a letter that would curl your hair! She said how they broke her daughter's heart and 'How could you do this to fans?' and things like that. A few weeks later, my dad got a call in his office. We still don't know how this happened. They said, 'We just opened up a bunch of new seats on the field. Do you want them?' So I ended up with better seats than I would have gotten. And I owe it all to Mom."

"Over the years, my parents have put up with a lot from me. I dedicated my first book, *Michael Jackson FAQ*, to them. The dedication reads 'They never told me to turn the music down.'"

Recipe Records

"Let It Brie," "I Am the Eggs Man": cheesy titles, you may say. That was exactly the idea when lifelong Beatles fan Lanea Stagg published *Recipe Records: A Culinary Tribute to The Beatles; 50 Recipes to*

Celebrate 50 Years. The book is filled with scrumptious recipes donated by fellow fans, authors, tour guides, and experts, from Liverpool to Walnut Ridge, who all wanted to be part of the "Fab food fun." Lanea's biggest supporter on the project was Jude Southerland Kessler, who as noted has written an entire series on John Lennon in novel form.

Lanea Stagg, 2016.

Even the table of contents in *Recipe Records* has a creative flair. "The Opening Act (Appetizers)" is where you'll find goodies such as "Little Piggies in a Blanket," "Hamburg Kraut Balls," and "Backstage Passes." For salads and side dishes, check out "You Say Goodbye, I Say Jell-O," while "Roadies" offers recipes for breads such as "Tangerine Tree & Marmalade Sky Bread." "Headliners" are entrees, including "Lady Medallions." Under "The Mosh Pit," Lanea lists recipes for "Get Back Joe Spiced Coffee," "George Martinis," and an assortment of other beverages. The list goes on and on until "The End," which offers suggestions to help you decide what to do with leftovers.

The idea to make recipes out of Beatles songs came to her out of the blue, Lanea said. She was at work, drowning out the Muzak by listening to The Beatles on her iPod, when she heard George sing about creme tangerine on "Savoy Truffle." "I thought *What the heck? He's singing about chocolate!* There it is. I came up with four truffle recipes: Smoot Mellow Toffee for George, Sweet Cherry Cream for Paul, Raspberry Nut for Ringo, and Lemon Tart for John. I made the flavors to fit their personalities."

Lanea used her family as guinea pigs. They tasted billions of recipes, she joked. "I tested out all the different ways of making truffles!"

Included with every recipe in the book are anecdotes and trivia about the songs and the band. Lanea said, "I wanted it to be something people would say they didn't know about that song or about The Beatles. Some people get oversaturated with 'She Loves You.' They don't realize there's a whole other level of The Beatles. I want them to experience The Beatles in a more obscure way and love them even more, like I do."

Lanea's love for cooking and her love for The Beatles are coinciding passions that began in childhood. "If you like to cook, you like to eat," she said. "When you really like good food, you try to figure out how to make that. That makes you a really good eater. When I was a little bitty girl, my mom taught me how to make little things like scrambled eggs or toast. I always liked to cook. I remember also as a little bitty girl, my dad played Beatles records. It's pretty much a simultaneous passion."

The *Recipe Records* tribute to The Beatles was not Lanea's first musical cookbook. Her first was with her best friend Maggie McHugh, who was a DJ in St. Louis and a huge Beatles fan.

"We were always thinking of clever things to do. It was her idea. We both loved music and food. We created a '60s edition of *Recipe Records*, naming recipes after songs or bands. It did really well. We decided to write another one. About a year after the first book came out, at age 44—we were the same age—she got sick and passed away. It was a shock and a life changer. About a year after she died, I decided to pick myself up and work on it again. Right when I was getting it to the printer, a marketing person called and said it was the 50th anniversary of The Beatles coming to America, and I should write a cookbook to honor them." Lanea was working full time, but she would stay up dreaming up recipes and titles all night long and had The Beatles cookbook published in 30 days.

In addition to writing the books, Lanea enjoys selling them herself. "I get a lot of satisfaction in connecting with the reader," she said. "That validates what you're creating. I love making friends with people that buy the books. That strengthens me as a human as well as a businessperson and a creative person. There's a lot of ugly in the world. It's not a bad thing to be your own promoter."

Lanea's love for The Beatles started when she was an infant. To soothe the fussy baby, her dad put a transistor radio next to her crib.

"I grew up listening to the radio all night long until I went to college. I know really random stuff. I can name songs and artists. When we get bored in the car, my husband puts on the radio and quizzes me. If the song is from the '50s to the '90s, I know it. But I really fell in love with music because of The Beatles. Now when I go to Beatlefests, I'm in the same company. I get the chance to talk with other music geeks!"

Lanea is the cochair of the Beatles at the Ridge symposium in Walnut Ridge, Arkansas. She used to attend Abbey Road on the River in

Louisville, Kentucky, with her daughter Abby, Margaret, and Margaret's niece. It is five days long with 100 tribute bands. But since Margaret passed, it has been too painful for Lanea to go back.

Over the last 20 years, Lanea's kids have howled along with "Hey Bulldog." When her daughter was little, she didn't know what the words meant, but she thought "Why Don't We Do It in the Road?" was so funny. She would scream it in the car.

"I loved watching them [her kids] experience The Beatles," Lanea said. "I kept falling deeper and deeper in love with them. The older I get, the more music I hear, I realize how important their contribution was. There's a lot of really junky music out there. A lot of the really good musicians were inspired by The Beatles."

Lanea says that her "love for The Beatles keeps me bonded with my girls. It's a very powerful connection. The songs take us back to all the good times we had" ... and, of course, bring back memories of her best friend, Margaret.

An Astounding Collection

Beatles book and autograph collector
with more than 1,000 books and hundreds
of autographs of the lads and other Beatles insiders.

No one forgets their first—especially not collectors. Proud owner of more than 1,000 Beatles books and treasures, John Bezzini of Connecticut fondly remembers his first print purchase: *The Real True Beatles Magazine* by Michael Braun in 1964. From that moment John was hooked, and to this day he still buys all of The Beatles print material he can find. When a new book comes out from a new angle, he is compelled to buy it, and new books are released every year. In each one he finds a little-known fact or quotes that he never heard before, inching him one step closer to completing the jigsaw puzzle that makes up The Beatles' story.

John's becoming an avid Beatles fan started with the music. John bought all their albums and 45s as they were released in the 1960s. As the Beatles' story progressed, he could clearly see that this band was special and was pushing the boundaries. That's when his obsession with print material caught on. He realized that The Beatles would be to music what Babe Ruth was to baseball.

John likened his addiction to a kid on a treasure hunt. It's the thrill of the search that fans his passion. Once he's found something new to

Ordinary Resolution of the Company of the Resolution above
set out notwithstanding that less than 21 days notice thereof
shall have been given.

Dated 20th December 1967.

Signed:

A document—a NEMS stock transfer—signed by Queenie and Clive
Epstein and each of The Beatles in December 1967 a few months after Brian
Epstein died. It was obtained by John Bezzini in a Sotheby's auction in the
1980s.

collect, he is on to find the next thing. His home resembles a museum,
with three rooms dedicated to his cache. In addition to the thousands
of books and magazines, he has all the music on vinyl, CDs, and DVDs.

Still, John insists that he isn't as obsessed as other collectors. He
does not feel the need to own all 16 versions of "No More Lonely Nights"
that Paul released, for instance—maybe just one or two—and he draws
the line at memorabilia such as Beatles soap and figurines. Everything
he buys has a purpose, he said. He can read the books—in fact, he has
read 99 percent of the books he owns—and he can enjoy all the music.

As you would expect of such a vast collection, John has many rare
and cherished items. He has books autographed by individual Beatles,
handwritten lyrics signed by Beatles children, records signed by producers, and more. His most prized possession, one purchased for only $500,
is a legal document signed by all four Beatles (on which Ringo signed
his legal name, Richard Starkey) as well as Queenie and Clive Epstein,
manager Brian Epstein's mother and brother. The document is a stock

transfer of NEMS, the record store owned by the Epsteins, to another party. John bought this at a Sotheby's auction in December 1967, just a few months after Brian Epstein died. He has since been offered a significant sum, but he would never part with the document. He is not into collecting for the money; in fact, he has never sold one item. The things he has bring him joy.

John grows his collection through research and relationships he has made throughout the years. He has books signed by three of The Beatles, individually and collectively. He has all except John Lennon.

When John Bezzini attended his first Beatlesfest in Boston in 1974, originally run by Joe Pope, publisher of the fanzine *Strawberry Fields Forever*, he bought George Harrison's autobiography *I, Me, Mine*, signed by George. John then learned about Genesis Publications, a publisher of signed and limited edition books. It was there that he was able to find other autographed books, including Ringo's *Postcards from the Boys* signed by Ringo and *The Polaroid Diaries*, a collection of Linda McCartney's photographs, signed by Paul. The closest John Bezzini has gotten to John Lennon's signature is an autographed copy of May Pang's book *Loving John*. May was in a relationship with John for 18 months when John and Yoko temporarily separated in 1973. This time period is famously called the "lost weekend."

John Bezzini also collects personal letters and signatures from people who had an important impact on the history and lives of The Beatles.

Julian Lennon and John Bezzini, 2017.

For instance, Ivan Vaughan was John Lennon and Paul's mutual friend when they were all teens. It was Ivan who introduced the two when John was performing with his first band, the Quarrymen. Later in life when Ivan was in the latter stages of Parkinson's disease, he wrote a book about living with the condition. John Bezzini has a book that Ivan signed to the person who did his taxes. The signature was verified by one of the Quarrymen. Another rarity is about 14 copies of a personal journal Paul McCartney wrote about the time he spent in a Japanese jail when he was arrested for marijuana possession. John has handwritten lyrics from Dhani Harrison's (George's son) latest album written on Dark Horse stationery. Dark Horse is the record label George Harrison founded.

Some of John's most treasured possessions are mementos of relationships he has forged. He has a personal connection to Julian Lennon, made when he sent Julian a copy of a rare recording called "That's My Life, My Love, and My Home," by Freddie Lennon, Julian's grandfather. John spent eight years tracking it down, and when he finally got it, he sent a copy to Julian's webmaster. He was told Julian would be extremely interested in it. Much to his surprise, John received a handwritten thank-you note from Julian.

Later, John went to Julian's book signing in Manhattan for a volume of a children's books trilogy Julian authored. John handed him a copy of a photo of Julian with his father on the set of the 1970s television show *Happy Days*. The photo was signed by one of the show's stars, Henry Winkler, whose character was famously nicknamed "the Fonz." Julian smiled and said, "Look, it's me and the Fonz." John also has Julian's handwritten lyrics to a song he never recorded.

John even has a letter that John Lennon's aunt Mimi, who raised him, sent to a fan. John Bezzini bought the letter from a man in Texas whom he now calls his friend. John has a sketch of Lennon from the late '50s by Helen Anderson too; Helen was in art school with Lennon, which is where he met Cynthia, his first wife.

Beatles fans are giving and love to share, John said. When he found an edition of a fan magazine he had spent years searching for, the fan who sent it to him would not accept money. She told him to donate to the animal shelter in her neighborhood instead. "That embodies a Beatles fan," he said.

Although John has a full-time job, he has found time to travel around the United States and Europe looking for pieces to add to his collection. Still looking for something new, he will often write to publishers asking to purchase signed books. He attends many conventions, and now he can find treasures much more easily online. He started a Facebook page, Beatles in Print—Together and Solo, and many Beatles authors have joined it.

John's next long-term project is to catalog his collection, which he plans to leave to his daughter or donate to a Beatles museum.

John embodies the spirit of The Beatles. When I admitted I was a bit jealous of his treasures, he said,

Part of the beauty of being a Beatles fan is not being jealous. One can be envious of some of the things that other collectors have, but ultimately we are all happy for what we are fortunate to have and what others may have that we may want but are unable to get. It is a communal feeling of happiness. Part of the joy of administering my Facebook page is bringing awareness to others of the many fabulous treasures that are out there to find. It's the feeling one gets when you give a gift. Often you get more pleasure from seeing the happiness you have brought to someone else.

And in the end, the love you take is equal to the love you make.

SEVEN

Inspired by the Magic

Probably every pop band and singer-songwriter since The Beatles has been influenced in some way by the boys who revolutionized the genre. Since it's not possible to talk with each and every one of them, I have spoken to two outstanding musicians.

Laurence Juber (LJ) was one of the lead guitarists for Wings. He has enjoyed an extremely successful career after playing with Paul's band. Some of LJ's life philosophies were inspired by the man himself.

Lucy Kaplansky never met or played with a Beatle, but she attributes her unique harmonizing style and her lyrical stories to our boys.

And Laurence Played the Guitar in the Band: LJ, Wings Lead Guitarist

Laurence "LJ" Juber is soft-spoken with a beautiful English lilt. Just like the melodies he plays soulfully on his guitar, you get lost in the cadence of his voice. But his words snap you back to attention. They are exhilarating.

LJ was lead guitarist with Wings from 1978 until the group disbanded in 1981. He had the privilege of performing with Wings to sold-out crowds during the band's UK tour in 1979. He was a member of the band through the recording of its last album, *Back to the Egg*. And he played on the smash hit "Good Night Tonight" as well as the number one single "Coming Up."

LJ describes his experience with Paul McCartney and Wings as a remarkable education.

"I always refer to it as getting my master's from McCartney University," LJ said. "I learned a lot about not only being in a remarkable band and working with a Beatle but also about the business of music and the creative side, because I never considered myself to be a writer."

Seven. Inspired by the Magic

LJ was a sought-after studio musician and a huge Beatles fan before joining the band.

"My contribution came from behind the music stand or in the context of coming up with guitar licks or solos to enhance a record, and there I was in a scenario where instead of doing three songs in a three-hour session we'd spend all day on one tune. The granular detail of it was so much more intense and creative. It was just an eye-opener for me."

As a member of Wings, LJ was often given the freedom to contribute.

"There were only a few scenarios where Paul had a specific guitar part that he wanted. There was an encouragement to make it feel like a band. We weren't just his hired guns. We really needed to think organically of it as a band, and that was good. The other thing of it, of course, is that if you look at the history of Paul as a writer-producer, there was never in The Beatles very much room for extended guitar solos. And that was true with Wings. You had to kind of pick your spots to make your statement. So, there was a certain kind of economy that went along with making that lead guitar contribution."

For LJ, a shining moment was when he proudly got to "put in his own voice" onstage in the iconic guitar solo on the classic "Let It Be."

"There wasn't in and of itself a definitive guitar solo because there were different versions of 'Let It Be' from The Beatles that had different guitar solos. So, that was an opportunity for me to put my voice in there. That was something I always tried to do as a studio musician was to give a little of my own personality, and there was certainly the opportunity to do that in Wings, just not on an extended basis."

Wings was still the period when Paul was kind of defining his own voice as opposed to being "Beatle Paul." Still, the band did play four Beatles hits on tour. They opened with "Got to Get You Into My Life," then sprinkled throughout the show they played "Fool on the Hill," "Let It Be," and "Yesterday."

"It was great [to play Beatles songs]. It still is great to play Beatles songs," LJ said. "I've done four albums of solo acoustic Beatles tunes. The thing about it is the integrity of the repertoire and the transcendence of that repertoire. There's so much resonance to those songs whether it was in Wings—I mean playing 'Let It Be' with Paul was just ... I mean how cool is that?! Being onstage with a Beatle is priceless, but at the end of the day the music itself is a transcendent thing. It's like asking what makes Shakespeare so special. It's something that is of its time and yet transcends its time."

155

LJ learned that Paul's creativity knew no bounds. He was always writing, working, and creating.

"I never really understood until then that you didn't have to wait for a bolt of lightning to slap you around," LJ said. "Paul would write a song over the weekend and come in Monday morning with 'Daytime Nighttime Suffering.' His ability to bring out that creativity, to sit down at the piano and come up with ideas or pick up a guitar, strum something, and turn it into a song, that was an enormously valuable experience for me, because it was like, okay, this is my job and that's his job. His job is to be creative. I've worked with artists who won't even write unless they have a record deal to write for. In Paul's case it was just a constant flow of creativity. You look back at The Beatles' history at how quickly *Sgt. Pepper* was released and the following week they're already working on *Magical Mystery Tour*. You can't keep him down. His creativity is constantly wanting to flow out."

Being around Paul and his late wife Linda inspired LJ not only musically but also on personal level. He described Paul and Linda's relationship as inseparable soulmates.

"The only time I ever saw them apart was when Paul was in jail in Tokyo after he got busted." LJ was referring to the time Paul was detained in Tokyo's Narita International Airport when he was found carrying nearly half a pound of marijuana in January 1980. His arrest thwarted plans for an 11-city concert tour. He was released nine days later and went home to England.

"They were very … just—they were a couple.... My wife Hope and I have really kind of taken our cue from this kind of couple consciousness that they had. Everything they did they did as a couple. Linda was very present. She was very much part of the decision making and part of the backing vocals or keyboard parts. That was true onstage as well as in the studio. She was very reliable and really had a very rock-and-roll sensibility."

Hope, a musician and screenwriter, shares LJ's passion for music and has produced a number of his solo albums.

The McCartneys' family style spilled over into the Jubers' protocol of always putting family first. At that time Paul and Linda had two kids, and the kids spent lots of time playing in the studio. When the band worked on the McCartneys' farm in Scotland, the kids were generally around. LJ and the rest of the band socialized with Paul, Linda, and the kids.

The day after Wings officially disbanded, LJ and Hope were met with a serendipitous chance that was set in motion when Hope accidentally bumped into Ringo Starr on the street in Beverly Hills. You can read more about their meeting in the chapter 4 interview with Hope Juber. Wings disbanded on April 27, 1981, and the future Jubers met on April 28, 1981. The couple tied the knot the following March, and as LJ puts it, Hope became pregnant on their wedding night.

"Coming out of Wings, I was starting to explore being in another band. [When Hope became pregnant] I realized that family was coming first," LJ said. "That again was a lesson from the McCartneys'."

LJ returned to his roots, studio work, with the Wings credit and two Grammys under his belt. He won his first Grammy Award with Wings and the second one was for an arrangement of the Pink Panther theme for solo guitar that was on an album that won best pop instrumental. That led him to playing on thousands of TV shows, records, and movies.

For the Jubers, the Beatles connection didn't stop when Wings disbanded. The family joyfully calls themselves "Beatles adjacent."

"Somehow in our household by virtue of being 'Beatles adjacent' there have been some moments that are almost cosmic in nature," LJ said. "They have touched our lives in so many ways, starting with the way Hope and I met through Hope's chance meeting with Ringo in Beverly Hills not long after John died. Then continued the day our younger daughter Ilsey was born in 1986. The day she was born I was due to be in the studio with George Harrison. Ilsey was born at 7:00 in the morning, and by noon I was in the studio with George. Hope was really disappointed because instead of 'Here Comes the Sun' it was 'Here Comes the Baby.' She was hoping to get to meet George that day. George got on the phone with Hope, and he said to come visit when she's ready. Two days later we go to visit him in a different studio with Ilsey, who's two days old in a baby carrier. George takes her out of the carrier and starts dancing around with her in the studio. At one point he touched her on the forehead and said something in Sanskrit [a language spoken mainly by Hindu priests]. We said, 'What did you do?' He said, 'I was so taken with this young life that I gave her the gift of music.'"

Now in her mid–30s, Ilsey Juber is a popular singer-songwriter who has written number one hits with Miley Cyrus, Beyonce, and Panic! at the Disco, just to name a few.

"George was very interesting to talk to because he talked about the fact that he wasn't one of the two front guys, so he kind of stood back a little bit from all of that, so that gave him a little objectivity," LJ said.

"He talked about his influences and how he got started playing. What was really cool at one point was I sang some backing vocals with him. Sharing a microphone with George Harrison ... and he said, 'Yeah, this is how Paul and I did most of the backing vocals on *Sgt. Pepper* because John wasn't as involved in that part of the production.' That was special stuff."

Eldest daughter Nico was always musical as well, but she took the corporate job route until she recently started writing a musical and realized that she hated her job so much she had to quit.

Nico had a thrilling experience meeting Paul with her parents when they visited in a recording studio years after the breakup of Wings. She was about 20 years old.

LJ described the scene.

"We were talking, and I noticed he [Paul] had a Hofner Bass, which was The Beatles' bass along with some other guitars I said, 'I see you're using a Hofner.' When we toured he was using a Yamaha Bass; he had stopped playing his Beatles bass. He said, 'That's not just any Hofner, that's *The* Hofner.' He walks over, picked it up, and he casually tossed it to Nico. She is standing there holding this bass ... and she's kind of slightly petrified. She was about 20. He took it back and then started to demonstrate how he played the bass line on 'Taxman.' That's very Paul to do that. Afterwards Hope said to Nico, 'Think of that experience like this—You're introduced to William Shakespeare, and he hands you his pen!'"

LJ recorded with two of the then three surviving Beatles when he worked with Ringo and Paul on Ringo's *Stop and Smell the Roses* album. "I worked with half The Beatles at once," LJ said, still agog.

For almost any musician, working with any of The Beatles would be a dream come true. But this is especially true for LJ. He was caught up with The Beatles frenzy as a 10-year-old in England in 1963. The Beatles were releasing singles every three months. "Please, Please, Me," then "From Me to You," then "She Loves You."

LJ turned 11 shortly after The Beatles did the Royal Command Performance in November 1963. He attributes that performance for royalty to giving the guitar more legitimacy and more gravitas. LJ's dad thought of the guitar as a hooligan instrument and wanted him to play the saxophone. It was around that time, November 1963, when the first Beatlemania wave crested in England.

"There was so much in the air," LJ recalled. "I got my first guitar when the album *Meet the Beatles* was released [in the States it was released as *With the Beatles*]. I remember getting my 32 shillings and 6x pence and standing outside the record store the day it was released to buy that album. 'I Want to Hold Your Hand' was the single that was coincidental with that, and it all reinforced my enthusiasm for playing the instrument. I was just enamored with it."

LJ played in wedding bands and top 40 bands as a teen. He studied guitar in high school and continued at London University. LJ joined the National Youth Jazz Orchestra, which he said was the farm team for studio work. He became a full-time studio musician playing on the BBC, records, and TV shows.

LJ was playing in the house band on a TV show with English pop star David Essex. Denny Laine—guitarist and one of the original founding members of Wings alongside Paul and Linda—was a guest on the show. At the time Wings was seeking a new guitar player, and Denny like LJ's style. Six months later LJ got the call from Paul's people while he was working in Studio 2 at Abbey Road—The Beatles studio.

"They said, 'Denny wants to know if you're available Monday to come and jam. Oh, by the way, Paul and Linda will be there."

A little panic set in. LJ didn't know any Wings songs and had to borrow albums from his brother, although he realized there was no way he'd be able to predict what he'd be called on to play. But there was no need to panic. It turned out they jammed on Chuck Berry tunes and Reggae groups.

"Paul wanted somebody versatile that could play a lot of different styles and was sober. I was professional about what I did. They offered me the job. There's a balance between being a professional musician and being a fan that is always kind of a delicate one. There's always a job to do, so you can't let the fandom overwhelm you."

Since Wings disbanded four decades ago, LJ has enjoyed a successful acoustic solo career. He has released more than two dozen albums, including four dedicated to Beatles music.

And That Bird Can Sing … and Write: Lucy Kaplansky

Popular singer-songwriter Lucy Kaplansky has had back-to-back hit albums with *Ten Year Night* and *Every Single Day*.

Personally, I discovered her in the late '90s when I saw her perform as part of a super–folk trio with Dar Williams and Richard Shindell called Cry, Cry, Cry. As a group they recorded some of their favorite songs written by other artists, which the *New York Times* dubbed a collection of lovely harmonizing and pure emotion. From there they enjoyed a national sold-out tour.

Since then, Lucy has enjoyed a lot of success as a solo artist and has toured internationally. What I love is her style; her lyrics hit me right to the core. What I didn't know was that one of my favorite folk artists attributes much of her musical storytelling and unique harmonizing style—which she is known for in the business—to The Beatles. I put two and two together when she posted on Facebook that she would be appearing on the Beatles Channel during Meg Griffin's show.

In our recent interview, Lucy said she has been singing for as long as she can remember. There was lots of music in the house, and her dad played the piano. But one of her first memories of loving music is The Beatles.

"We lived in England when I was five for a year, and I remember seeing them on TV on *Top of the Pops*. And it's funny, I remember thinking—I was five or six years old—something along the lines of 'They always tell a story in their songs,' which I guess was apparent to a five-year-old!"

It's no wonder that Lucy's songwriting style emulates The Beatles by weaving storytelling into her music. Her most popular song, "Ten Year Night"— cowritten with her husband Richard Litvin—is about the unusual way they met and connected. A more recent hit, "Old Friends," tells the story of her lifelong friendship and performing with Shawn Colvin.

When Lucy got older she discovered Joni Mitchell, a pioneer of singer-songwriters who launched an entire generation of songwriters who are women. Lucy was about 11 years old when she decided she wanted to be Joni Mitchell and started writing songs. Lucy's first songs were "really bad."

But Lucy persevered. While growing up in Chicago she kept writing and playing music, getting better all the time. As soon as she finished high school, she took the plunge and followed her dream to the New York music scene in the early '80s. She hit the jackpot when she started singing with Suzanne Vega and Shawn Colvin at one of the central music venues of the era—Folk City. Folk City is where Bob Dylan played his first gig, and *Rolling Stone* listed it as one of the three top music venues in the world along with The Cavern and CBGB.

"When I started, I very consciously imitated and aspired to write

Lucy Kaplansky, 2017.

like Steve Earle. And somebody years ago said to me 'Oh, you've been listening to Steve Earle, and Steve Earle has been listening to The Beatles!'"

Lucy could relate to that immediately.

"There's this tradition of the kinds of harmonic things they [The Beatles] did that have seeped into all kinds of people's music."

And it seeped into hers.

"I can think of one totally clear example. There's this one song of mine, 'Don't Mind Me,' that ends with the 4 minor [minor iv chord] which is just a very Beatles kind of thing. To end on that chord—it feels like they did it so many times."

Lucy listened to The Beatles religiously growing up. She had older brothers, and they loved The Beatles. And she remembers loving them since she was five in England. "Of course, in England they were the biggest thing in the world, just like in the US, and I listened from then on."

Lucy listened to the Red and Blue compilation albums so many times in her room growing up "that to this day I hear one of those songs, and I can start singing the next song in the sequence on the album in the key that it was in. It just imprinted on my brain."

Lucy doesn't know the actual Beatles albums as well. But she listened to the compilations "a gazillion times. It's just the most timeless, perfect music."

As an adult, Lucy appreciates The Beatles' music even more. She loves how simply complex their music is and the joy they took in creating and performing.

"First and foremost is the singing! Their harmonies, their incredible lead vocals. Their exuberance." She loves that their songs are more than pop songs. And just like when she was five, she still loves the way they tell stories "and just the harmonic brilliance!"

The songs are vocally intricate, and that had a direct impact on Lucy's style of singing harmony.

"What they are doing with the harmonies are complicated, unusual and unpredictable. Like 'If I Fell,' that's just incredible. Talk about an incredible harmony that would counterpoint—what they're doing is beautiful, and that kind of thing really influenced me. I love singing harmony and I'm known for singing harmony, and one of the things I'm known for is doing unpredictable, unusual things with the harmony. So case in point, 'If I Fell'—that's not what you expect to hear."

As a young girl learning guitar, Lucy quickly realized how much more there was to those songs than what appeared on the surface. The first song she learned was "Here Comes the Sun." Then she dove deeper.

"You don't realize how complicated some of these chord changes and melodies are until you try and sit down on a piano or guitar and try to reproduce them."

These days Lucy cowrites a lot of her songs with her husband Richard Litvin. And she's quick to point out that some ideas are his. But her ideas mostly come from a feeling or something that moved her. Her writing style is much like Paul McCartney's (the way Laurence Juber described Paul's writing style in another interview) in that she treats writing like a craft. She tries to write as often as she can. She writes when she is not necessarily feeling inspired, not necessarily when she's feeling anything. But she just sits down and tells herself it's time to work.

"And somehow this thing that moved me kind of comes out of my mouth. It's an unconsciously driven process. It's mysterious. Things come out of seemingly nowhere. So, I let whatever that process is just play through me, and low and behold, once in a while something good comes out. You kind of ride that wave until you need to edit or give up."

Lucy was also much more directly influenced by Paul McCartney when he played mandolin and ukulele at a concert she went to with her then eight-year-old daughter and her husband.

"He just kept switching instruments, and he was so great on all of them. My friend had given me a mandolin, and I hadn't done anything with it. [Watching Paul,] I thought I should teach myself a couple of chords on mandolin. So, that night inspired me to actually learn to play the mandolin. And then I ended up using it in all my shows and writing some songs with it."

That's not the only time Lucy saw Paul McCartney in person. She almost forgot to tell me that she saw "The Concert for George." How you forget something like that is beyond me. The story goes that her college professor husband was living in Dublin for the semester, and Lucy had a friend in the music business who had a connection. They had incredible seats. In fact, they were so close to the stage that for a moment in the video you can see them in the audience. She said the concert was truly magical, as the rest of us can only imagine.

"When Ringo and Paul were there together it was like seeing The Beatles.... And Dhani, in person, looked exactly like a young George. We could really see. We were right up in front. It was really great."

Even though Lucy has had these big Beatles moments, sometimes it's the little stories that get to her the most. She tours internationally, and when she plays in England it's always a thrill.

"I play in England a lot, and there's always people I meet who saw The Beatles play when they were first starting out. It's really cool. They tell me 'Oh, they played in this little church, and I was there.' That's always exciting. That doesn't happen in the US. Nobody saw them when they were starting out."

Lucy loves playing Beatles music in concert. She has recorded "I've Just Seen a Face" and "I'm Looking Through You." But "Let It Be" holds a special place in her heart.

"I really love singing 'Let It Be.' Before I read Bob Spitz's book *The Beatles*, it had never occurred to me that he [Paul] had written that about his mother. About losing his mother. I never thought of it that way. I thought it was Mary—Mother of God. When I lost my mother 12 years ago it really meant a lot to me, and it still does."

And that daughter Molly—that little girl she brought to Paul's concert—she 19 now and a huge fan herself. "Every generation discovers The Beatles," Lucy said when talking about her daughter. "We played The Beatles for her in the car. We spent a lot of time in the car—they would come to shows with me. She just loved them. I guess we must have turned her on to them, and then she just went to town."

While Molly is not a singer in the band, she plays lots of instruments and has learned "a zillion" instrumental parts on Beatles songs. She plays the drums, the guitar, and keyboards and produced a video of herself on all the instruments on a Beatles song for a school project.

"That's interest beyond the normal interest, I think," Lucy said.

As far as Lucy goes, her journey to a successful music career was long, winding, and bumpy complete with twists and turns. At 23 she was starting to have some real success. She was written about in the *New York Times* as an up-and-coming new artist and someone to watch. But she wasn't ready for it. She dropped out of the music scene and got a PhD in psychology. What she learned from working as a psychologist and seeing a therapist of her own was that she was "neurotically conflicted." She realized she was running away from what she really wanted. Nearly a decade later at age 32, she came back to music. It was the scariest thing she had ever done. She had no illusion that she would necessarily be successful. But music was her true passion, and she was going to see it through; she was not going to quit again.

Like the Beatles, Lucy followed her dream until that long and winding road led to a dream come true.

EIGHT

Sgt. Pepper Taught the Band to Play

For millions of fans like me who are too young to have ever seen The Beatles perform or remember them on *The Ed Sullivan Show*, nothing beats a great tribute band. The good ones transport you to a time and place you can only dream of, and the *really* good ones bring back fond memories to those who were there.

It takes a strong passion to want to become a Beatle and an even stronger talent to realize it onstage.

Beatles Tribute Bands Pop Up Everywhere, Even Slovenia

There's a popular tribute band in Slovenia, Help! A Beatles Tribute, founded by a guy from—wait for it—New Jersey. It was a long and winding road that led Ernie Mendillo, Paul in the band, to Slovenia and a twisty-bendy road that led him to his split-second encounter with Paul McCartney.

Ernie's band Help! A Beatles Tribute became a European sensation after getting its big break playing International Beatleweek in Liverpool. They have toured 20 countries, including Greece, Spain, Sweden, and Norway. Their biggest markets are Germany, Switzerland, Holland, France and, of course, Slovenia. Ernie and the band just got back from Bahrain, off the coast of Saudi Arabia, the day we had our transatlantic phone call. So, it's no wonder that Oto Pestner, an enormously famous singer in Slovenia—think Frank Sinatra—contacted Ernie hoping that he had a connection with the real Paul. Oto wanted to get his recordings to Paul.

"I didn't, but we became friendly, and he even sang a few songs at some shows as our musical guest."

Oto persevered in his quest to meet Paul. He sent letters to Paul's production company with no reply. Oto went straight to the top and asked the president of Slovenia to write a letter to Paul that included recordings of Oto singing the entire *Sgt. Pepper* album in Slovene and asking Paul to perform at a 60th birthday celebration for Oto.

"The story goes that after Paul had to cancel dates in Japan due to illness, he was in his London office and asked his secretary 'what have you got'? She told him he had a letter from the president of Slovenia. He told her to put it on his desk with the other interesting mail. Paul read it, and his secretary contacted Oto! Unfortunately, arrangements couldn't be made for a concert appearance, but Oto stayed in contact with his office."

Ernie Mendillo and Paul McCartney, 2016.

A couple of years later, 2016 to be exact, Oto made arrangements to perform in Munich on the same date Paul was to appear at the stadium there. Oto was able to secure tickets to the concert, the sound check, and backstage passes. But he was stuck! Munich is a four-hour drive from Slovenia, and Oto can't drive a car. He called his friend Ernie to drive and be his plus one to all the events that night, including the chance to come face to face with Paul McCartney. Ernie jumped at the offer.

"We made it backstage, and I was surprised. There were only 20 or 30 people back there as guests. Klaus Voorman was sitting at a table with his sons. I was dying to go and talk to him, but I didn't. I didn't want to impose. Abe Laboriel [Paul's drummer] and Brian Ray [Paul's lead guitarist] came into the room. At one point Brian actually came over to introduce himself. We chatted for a bit, and Oto mentioned that I am in a Beatles tribute band. That was embarrassing!"

Then a representative escorted them to an area to meet Paul shortly before he hit the stage. They were told only that the staff photographer would take a photo and there would be no selfies or autographs. Ernie was disappointed because he had his parents mail him his *Meet the Beatles* album all the way from New Jersey, hoping Paul would sign it. Ernie's disappointment did not last long.

"We waited patiently while the room was cleared out. Security was incredibly tight. They operated like the Secret Service protecting the president! Klaus and his family were taken into Paul's dressing room, but all the other guests left without meeting him. We were the last two people in the room when the representative reappeared and escorted us down a hallway. There was a backdrop and a photographer, and we were told Paul would be out shortly. I chatted with the photographer and asked how many people get to do this, and he said only two or three per show. In fact, Klaus Voorman and his family were the only other people that took a picture with him that day."

All conversation stopped when ...

"Suddenly, from around a corner, Paul appeared with a few of his people. He looked quite sharp in his stage clothing and was walking straight toward us. He shook our hands and said hello. He said he heard we were from Slovenia. Oto replied yes and that we were hoping someday he would perform there. He said

Help! A Beatles Tribute re-creating the famous record cover for the BBC, walking in London. This picture was actually taken in 2016 in Kranj, a small town in Slovenia. Left to right, Matic Pelcel (John), Gasper Oblak (the band's former Ringo), Ernie Mendillo (Paul), and Ziga Stanonik (George). Their current drummer is Anze Semrov (courtesy Ernie Mendillo).

maybe and asked if we were ready to take the photo. We then turned to the camera and took the shot. He shook our hands again and said, 'Enjoy the show,' and off he went. You could have knocked me over with a feather! It was one of the greatest moments of my life! I've been a fan since I was four and growing up in New Jersey. I never thought I would meet one of The Beatles. It was literally a dream come true! To this day I still can't believe it!"

Ernie's earliest musical memory is hearing "I Want to Hold Your Hand" as a four-year-old in New Jersey. His dad was a Beatles-loving math teacher just 31 years old. He brought the albums home for Ernie and his brothers to hear.

"They were fresh and exciting. I don't remember anything else from the time. They were my first impression of rock music." Ernie was mesmerized by Paul and at 15 began playing bass.

"I dove into it," he said. "I went through all the albums and never stopped." A few years later in the mid–'80s he played bass in a popular New York band, The Brandos. The band got a record deal, had videos on MTV, and went on American and European tours. It was in Austria where Ernie met his first wife; she was Slovenian. She moved to New York. In 1998, married with two children, the young family packed up and moved to Slovenia. Ernie remained in The Brandos for a few more years. Unfortunately, that marriage didn't work out. The good news is that Ernie stayed on in Slovenia and is happily remarried with two more children.

In 2012 he was playing in a band and was approached by the British embassy in Slovenia. They asked for an all–Beatles show for a Lions Club event. It was a smash hit. Then they got into the costumes and studied the music, and the band played on.

In 2015 the band played International Beatleweek in Liverpool, and the rest is history. Earlier that same year the band played at a birthday party in Moscow for one of the richest men in the world, Russian billionaire Mikhail Prokhorov, who once owned the Brooklyn Nets.

Ernie was the first tribute band musician I had spoken to who played in Manama, the capital of Bahrain.

"It was surreal," Ernie said. "A million and a half people live there. There are ex-patriots from all the world, England, the Philippines, Egypt, Cashmere, everywhere. The people are very open and incredibly polite. It's unbelievably safe. You could leave your phone on the table, and no one would touch it. But it's also like the Las Vegas of the Middle

East. [There's lots of live music and dancing.] People love living there. It's a better lifestyle. I didn't know what to expect. I had to look it up on a map."

That's one of the things Ernie loves most about playing in the band. He gets to see places he otherwise would never have the opportunity to see. He meets all kind of happy, friendly people who direct him to the local spots, outside of the tourist sights. He gets to really know unique places all over Europe.

No matter where Help! A Beatles Tribute goes, no matter what the country's native language, whether or not the audience speaks English, everyone knows all the words to The Beatles' songs, and they get on their feet and sing and dance.

That's the magic of music. That's the magic of The Beatles.

The Other Wildly Popular Fab Four

You can still see Paul; you can still see Ringo. But what you can't see if you were born too late is the four Beatles together onstage. For that, you've got to see the next best thing: the Fab Four, one of the most popular Beatles tribute bands in the world.

"Until you can put on 3D glasses and see virtual Beatles, I think people will always want to see flesh and blood and have real people talking to them and see people singing live," said Ron McNeil, the Fab Four's founder.

The Fab Four got their start 25 years ago in a local bar in suburban Orange County, California. From there they rose to international fame. They're on the top of the bill at International Beatleweek, the largest annual Beatles happening in the world, with 70 tribute bands from 20 countries playing at all the popular Beatles venues and taking it to the streets of Liverpool, where all four Beatles were born and got their start as a band. When they're not at Beatleweek, the Fab Four play all over the United States and Mexico.

It all started as a dream for John imitator Ron, born and raised in Orange County. He was too young to be an original fan. His obsession started in the '70s when he began borrowing his sister's records and never gave them back. As soon as heard those songs, the only thing he ever wanted to do was play Beatles music.

Ron did more than simply listen; he studied. He learned every lyric and every guitar lick backwards and forwards. He started with their voices until he could easily pick out who was singing on each track. Soon he was able to pick out not only the chords but also what types of guitars they were using. The next thing he did was pick up a guitar and play, imitating everything they did. Almost everything.

"The Beatles did their thing. They were a band. They wrote music. Then it was over," Ron said. "People don't understand all of the by-products of when they came out. They obviously changed music. They were writing their own songs when bands just didn't do that. There was never a group that had four singers."

And the way they looked was way beyond compare. "They changed fashion. They looked different. That was their own creation, other than getting a little nudge from [Beatles manager] Brian Epstein to change their image. Their hair was their idea. Then when they grew their mustaches and grew their hair long, that was all them."

Ron was just a toddler when The Beatles played the Hollywood Bowl. He was just hitting puberty when the band broke up. He never got the chance to see them live, but his obsession was powerful. His dad took him to the next best thing when he was a teen: *Beatlemania*, a Broadway show featuring four guys who were not The Beatles playing Beatles music note for note while looking and acting like the originals. Experiencing changing costumes with the band's changing times while images of the era played behind them onscreen was the

The Fab Four, with Andy Sarraf (kneeling) as Paul McCartney, Joe Bologna as Ringo, Adam Hastings as John (seated in chair), and Gavin Pring as George (right), 2018.

170

ultimate Beatles experience. The touring company played in Los Angeles in the late '70s. For Ron, it was a life changer.

"It left a huge impression on me," Ron said, "I thought maybe one day I could grow up to be a Beatle."

Ron sat on his idea for many years. In those days, there were lots of Elvis impersonators. Remember when a gaggle of them flew in formation from parachutes over the skies? Everyone was getting married by Elvis in Vegas. Maybe there were too many Elvi. But there wasn't anything else. It wasn't like it is today, where you can find Bon Jovi and Queen tribute bands in every corner bar.

Life went on for Ron, but the *Beatlemania* image was indelible on his young mind. Years later, he attended a Beatles convention in nearby Los Angeles, and that changed his life forever. It was there that he met the Paul to his John.

Ron was mesmerized by a chubby kid named Ardy Sarraf, who was not dressed like a Beatle and played a right-handed (Paul is famously lefty) Yamaha bass guitar during the battle of the bands at the convention. "He was playing 'Coming Up' by Paul McCartney, and literally the hair on the back of my neck went straight up," Ron said. "I could not believe this guy was sounding exactly like Paul McCartney. It was like some kind of weird trick."

The meeting between Ron and Ardy was charged, just like when 17-year-old John Lennon met 15-year-old Paul McCartney on July 6, 1957, at the Woolton Parish Church Garden Fete (Party) in Liverpool, where John and was playing with the Quarryman. Ardy learned to play the bass upside down and backwards. The team found David Brighton, who became their George, and Rolo Sandoval as Ringo. The band has had many iterations since the beginning; most recently, Gavin Pring took over as George, and Joe Bologna took over as Ringo.

Following in their idols' footsteps, the tribute band started small. Their first gig was at Music City in Orange County, owned by Bill Medley, one of the Righteous Brothers. It was a place where locals and popular musicians from the '60s played. The Fab Four landed a slot every Tuesday night. The first couple of Tuesdays were abysmal. If the "crowd" reached 30, that was a lot.

Word got around, though, and by the fourth week there was a line out the door. The band moved on up the food chain to a British pub in Los Angeles, the land of broken dreams, and they proved to be one of the lucky few. The crowds started to grow and grow. With the momentum building, they were contacted by a promoter in Las Vegas—the big time. Now the act was gelling. A Vegas audience demanded more. The band answered. They were more than four guys playing Beatles tunes; they were a four-headed monster. They became showier, they were funny between songs, and there were costume changes just like what Ron saw at *Beatlemania*. "We started to turn our little club band into more of a show," Ron said. "I think that's where it started to take off."

When they got the call to play Beatleweek for the first time, Ron was on cloud nine. His time in Liverpool gave Ron a deeper understanding of the lads themselves:

> Staying in the hotel and hearing the Livabirds early in the morning and getting that feel of just being in that kind of an older city made me relate to who they were. I've been in LA my whole life, so it was just a great feeling. Hearing all those Liverpudlian accents all around, you got the feeling that the guys were just kids blowing through their town, trying to make music together. I don't think they really understood the impact they had on people. It was like a meteor; they just really shook the planet. I'm happy to be a part of it. It is a little bizarre at times, but what a great job it is to have. People who didn't grow up with The Beatles get to see what the music sounds like in a live performance. That's our job—my only job for 25 years.

The Fab Four became so popular that in 2013 they won an Emmy for their PBS special *The Fab Four—The Ultimate Tribute*. It still runs on PBS stations across the country today.

After all these years, many more than the real Beatles performed, the Fab Four's show is so tight and so well orchestrated that new tribute bands coming up in the current decade emulate it instead of looking directly to The Beatles. "'Britain's Finest' do a great Fab Four show," one review said of a new tribute band. "'Hard Day's Night' is the best tribute to the Fab Four you're going to see," said another.

Instead of using The Beatles' formula, other tribute bands use the Fab Four's formula. The Beatles opened all their shows with "Twist and Shout," whipping the crowd into a frenzy. They played for only 20 minutes, and that energy held strong. The Fab Four's shows are much longer, so they must build to a crescendo.

"We had to learn what songs to open and close with and what to say between songs to keep the audience with us," said Ron. "Groups in England and all around the world have copied our formula. They play the same songs in the same order and say the same things. It's cool. It took us a long time to develop it, but at least people see the value in writing a good show. It's flattering."

The Fab Four are so popular that they easily fill 1,500-seat theaters and are often double-booked. In fact, they had to expand to include eight more members to form three sets of four to keep up with the demand. When they are wanted in Iowa and Mexico on the same night, it all works. No one is left disappointed.

The Fab Four have even played at celebrity events. Paul Stanley, lead singer of Kiss, saw them at House of Blues in LA and hired them for his birthday party, and they played for Foo Fighters' lead singer Dave Grohl's wedding. They met the real Paul McCartney himself. Paul McCartney said to Gavin Pring, the current George, "You even look a bit like George."

Summoning George's sharp wit, Gavin replied, "You look a bit like Paul."

And in the end, it's the music that pulls it all together now. It bridges gaps and entertains people ages 8 to 80. Grandparents bring their grandchildren.

As it did in the '60s, the music bridges racial divides and crosses language barriers. In 1964 at the height of Beatlemania, the band was booked to play Florida's Gator Bowl in Jacksonville. Five days before the show the lads learned that the audience was segregated, and they refused to play. They released a statement that read "We will not appear unless Negroes are allowed to sit anywhere." The Beatles won their battle, and the stadium was integrated.

Of course, The Beatles have played worldwide tours as a group and as solo performers. The result is that non–English speakers sing along to all the songs. In my interviews for this book, people from non–English-speaking countries have told me they learned the language through early Beatles tunes. And now creatures across the universe will become familiar with The Beatles' songs. NASA's Deep Space Network beamed the song "Across the Universe" directly into deep space at 7 p.m. EST on February 4, 2020.

"What's more fulfilling than having everybody sing along to all those great songs?" Ron said. "From kids to old people, everyone's smiling. There's no better job in the world."

Beatlemania

Beatles tribute on Broadway.

"I hate The Beatles. They ruined my life!" George once said in an interview. Of course, he was joking.

And, well, maybe it wasn't the George you're thinking of. This George's real name is Pete Santora, who portrayed George Harrison in the original *Beatlemania* on Broadway in the '70s and then went on to do a national tour of the show. You never know, it could have been Pete Santora who Ron McNeil of The Fab Four saw onstage in Los Angeles.

To this day, Pete plays a tribute show of George's music called "A Night of George" to commemorate the Beatle's birthday. Pete jokes that the band ruined his life because they have been a part of his life almost for as long as he can remember.

Pete wasn't influenced only by George but rather by each of them. "When I play at my local gigs, I cover songs by all of them." Pete writes, plays, and records his own music, all because of the band's inspiration.

Pete was listening to The Beatles before they even hit *The Ed Sullivan Show*.

> I used to hang around a record shop when I was about 13. The owner played "My Bonnie" by Billy Sheridan. He told me, "Those guys that play backup are really great. They're gonna be a big deal." That's the first I heard of them. "I Want to Hold Your Hand" had been out in '63 and "She Loves You" before that.
>
> It was when I was sitting in front of the TV that I saw how great they were. Like many of my friends I said, "Let's put a band together." I was already playing guitar. I saw George, and I wanted to play like him. He was doing all that solo stuff, and he was the lead.

Pete loved that the band seemed to be having so much fun.

In the mid–'60s Pete was in a band in the Bronx that had a professional record deal, but The Beatles were still "it" for him. "They put out records one after another that were just great. In the old days, you would get an album where there were maybe one or two good songs. All their music was so well written and so well recorded. It was so much fun. It was great to be able to copy them."

All of this led to Pete Santora becoming his idol, George Harrison, in full costume, singing and playing just like him in *Beatlemania* on Broadway in the 1970s. "It fulfilled a dream," Pete said. "I even got to go to London in 1979 for a show. I was very lucky to be able to get involved."

Personally, George was something of a role model for Pete. George was someone who had a deep spirituality. And of course, his playing was wonderful. There was so much to learn from him.

Pete has opened for Pete Best's band at the Cavern and the Casbah.

"I'm close to that scene over there," Pete Santora said. "It's almost like I'm an honorary Liverpudlian." One of his special Liverpool memories is of singing "Within You Without You" at the city's largest cathedral for a special event.

Pete casually talked about the instances when he met each of The Beatles in person, which culminated with the hour he spent with his idol in San Francisco in 1967. "I ran into John a couple of times when I lived in the city [New York]," he said. "We met on the street and said hello. When I went to England to Wembley Stadium, I briefly met McCartney. These weren't long meetings. They were just saying hello and getting introduced. I met Ringo at a signing in the city [New York]. My friend runs *Modern Drummer* magazine, and he is fast friends with Ringo. He told me he's a warm and wonderful guy."

Then came the big event, which Pete still talks about in a very low-key tone:

"I met George in San Francisco in 1967. I had gone out there to the Summer of Love. I was in Golden Gate Park when he was there, and a group of us hung out with him for an hour or so. He just showed up. We met on the street. We walked down to Golden Gate Park with him, Patty [Boyd], and Derek [Taylor]. As we were walking with them, more and more people realized who it was. The crowds got bigger and bigger. We told them they should get out of here. He was very nice. We were telling him how much he meant to us. *Sgt. Pepper* had just come out, and we told him how much we loved it. Someone gave him a guitar, and he started strumming it. He didn't play songs, just chords and strumming. He wasn't giving a concert."

I asked Pete what it was like to meet his idol.

"He was my hero ... and there he was. Unfortunately, George didn't have a warm feeling when remembering that afternoon when he was interviewed about it years later. His comments were not very nice about the people there. He didn't like the hippie thing. He called them 'dirty hippies.' You know, he was getting out of that thing. His spiritual thing was on another road. He was off with Ravi Shankar; he wasn't into that hippie thing."

Knowing how George felt does not take away from Pete's fond memories of spending an hour with his hero.

These days, Pete still hears new stories and sees new pictures of the band. He knows people who worked for Apple. "The music is still fabulous! The songs themselves were so good, so honest, so well recorded. Their recordings are some of the best recordings ever made. Even today, almost 50 years later, they sound great. They were recorded so well by George Martin. He was a godsend for them."

I told Pete about *Beat Bugs*, the Netflix show for toddlers set to Beatles music. He wasn't aware of it, but he wasn't surprised. "John would love that," he said. "Some of those songs are very easily adaptable for kids. They have a childlike quality, an innocence to them in addition to all their worldliness."

In Pete's eyes, as in the eyes of everyone else I interviewed, The Beatles are eternal. "My generation brought up their kids on Beatles songs," Pete said. "They are songs and stories that everyone can relate to. There's always something there."

He Walked Out of Our Dreams

Clark Gilmour could have walked right out of a 1960s fan magazine full of the young Beatles' faces. His Liverpudlian accent completes the dream. It's no wonder that when lucky Beatles fans get to watch Clark perform at the Cavern Club, where he plays John Lennon in Them Beatles and where he's a resident musician, they get lost in the fantasy that they're actually seeing a Beatle.

Clark hails from Scotland, but he's been in Liverpool so long he could easily be mistaken for a native. He may play John, but to me he's a Paul double. Clark even sports the haircut, not a wig. On top of being a resident musician, he's also the band liaison at the Cavern Club, vetting bands to perform at International Beatleweek. "It's all Beatles all the time," Clark says with his adorable lilting accent. "It couldn't get any better than this."

Now in his 30s, life for Clark wasn't always like this, but it was a not so long and winding road that got him here. Back in Scotland his dad, Lawrence, was a Paul McCartney impersonator. In fact, he was a body double for Paul in one of his videos. "He had a full-time job," Clark said. "The Beatles band was a part-time gig that he would do on Fridays and Saturdays. When I got to a certain age, I would go with him. I got to meet lots of musicians from the '60s like the Searchers, the Mersey Beats. I was always going to see them at the fests. When I finished uni [university], my future was either teaching or starting a tribute band."

What's a fella to do? Clark "put adverts out and hung flyers at music shops." His soon-to-be partner, Jerry, answered an ad, and it turned out they already knew each other from the music scene in Glasgow. From

Clark Gilmour on stage at the Cavern Club, 2016.

there it was a joint effort, and the band took off like wildfire. They played in 30 different countries, including Australia, New Zealand, and Singapore. Then they got chosen to play Beatleweek in the Beatles mecca, Liverpool. "Living in Liverpool was always in the back of my mind," Clark said. "I've always loved coming here and playing the fest. And I'm a massive Liverpool football—what you call soccer—fan."

Clark was offered the gig in Liverpool when his wife was pregnant with their first child. "It was not on the agenda to move to a new country. But when there's a big change in your life, you think maybe it's time to make a big change."

Clark and his pregnant wife packed up their belongings, headed to their new life in Liverpool, and never looked back. Now the couple has a son and a daughter. "Both kids learned to go 'Yeah, yeah, yeah,'" he chuckled. "I always play guitar in the front room, and my little girl used to call it 'the yeah yeah' because she associated it with 'She Loves You.' My boy is obsessed with the guitar."

When Clark is not performing, he is occupied with his liaison job. "Being band liaison is a busy ordeal," he said. "I'm constantly bombarded by everything—emails, phone calls, messages at 2 a.m. from South America. It's round the clock. It's cool to be in touch with these people that are trying to come to the mecca."

So, what appeals to someone who hears from Beatles bands all over the world? "There are bands that dress, sing, and talk like The Beatles. Fans love that," Clark said. "I also look for bands that play with a different twist."

There's a band called the Funkles that plays Beatles music in a funky style. There are acoustic bands, ukulele bands, and the Fab Faux, who are amazing but don't do the costumes and the accents. Some bands play really heavy versions of "Come Together" and "Helter Skelter."

The bands just keep pouring in. "We get about 200 to 300 applications [to play during Beatleweek] a year," Clark said. "Those are just the ones that fill out the official application. We have to narrow it down to 70 bands from about 20 countries. What's amazing is about 95 percent of the bands have a good grasp of English. A lot of them learned it through The Beatles and their music. Just the opposite of that, Japanese bands are meticulous with the music and all the words, but they come in with a translator."

But it's not Europe or Japan or even America that boasts the biggest number of applications to play the fest. Just as Cavern City Tours codirector Bill Heckle said, The Beatles are huge in Brazil. "A lot of Latin America is passionate about The Beatles," Clark said, "especially the Brazilians. Maybe it's the sheer size of the place. Maybe it's because they're emotional people; they're passionate about soccer too. Or it could be because Paul McCartney did a gig there about 20 years ago, and that was the first-ever Beatle in South America. There's a new generation reaping the benefits. We have 10 bands from Brazil."

Even when there are lulls in bands clamoring to play the fest, Clark loves his life at the Cavern Club. "It's insane," he said happily. "It's all centered around the Cavern. We are a live music venue. We have music playing 13 hours a day, 7 days a week."

"The Beatles are one of the biggest brands in the world. Long may it continue. I hope in 50 years' time, people are still talking about The Beatles."

Liverpool Shuffle

How Paul in a tribute band is on a first-name basis
with the real Sir Paul.

"'How ya doing, Freddy G?' That's what Paul knows me as," Freddy Giovanelli says with a big grin on his face. He loves to talk about his friendship with Sir Paul. Freddy, an Italian guy with a thick Brooklyn accent, immediately takes you into his inner circle. "To him I was a nice kid, a runner that took care of things. He knew me by name—Freddy, Freddy G." That's one of the amazing stories Freddy—bass player who sings all Paul's songs for the New York Beatles tribute band Liverpool Shuffle—told.

Freddy was just a kid in his mid–20s when he worked with Paul and his band for four years, 1988 through 1991. Oh, the stories he loves to tell. I'm sure some people don't believe him. He says his own brother was skeptical until many years later when he saw Paul McCartney shake Freddy's hand and put a hand on his shoulder, saying in his way "How'ya doing, my friend?"

Freddy was struck by lightning—or maybe won the lottery is a better way to say it—when he got to work for Paul. "It's 1988. I'm working for Sam Ash [a music store] on 46th Street in Manhattan," Freddy said.

Liverpool Shuffle, with Brian James, the late Freddy Giovanelli, Joe Refano, and Jamie Bateman in 2016.

179

Freddy knew Ron Delsner, who was known for promoting concerts in the New York tristate area in the '60s, '70s, '80s, and '90s. Ron would call Freddy and ask for guitar parts and other equipment for shows he was working on. "One day he calls and needs some equipment to rent for a week or two," Freddy said. "He's at the Lyceum Theatre two blocks away. So, I load up a hand truck and go. I go in through a side door and walk right onstage with the hand truck. I look up, and I make eye contact with Paul McCartney! He's behind the piano with the full band behind him. I make eye contact just before he's starting to play 'Live and Let Die.' They're in full dress. I just froze. 'Oh my God.' I put the amp down and said, 'Keith, can I please stay?'" Amazingly, Keith said yes—as long as Freddy promised to sit in a corner and be quiet. "So I sat in the chair," Freddy said. "I had to pee so bad, but I wouldn't move."

After a while, the band broke for lunch. There was a big round table for about 10 or 12 people. All of the food was vegetarian, Freddie remembered. "Tofu meatballs, stuff like that," he said. "Just then, Wix Wickens [keyboard player for Paul] comes over to me and says, 'I'm Wix. How'ya doin?' I said, 'I'm Fred. I work for Sam Ash.' He invited me to eat!"

Thrilled, Freddy filled a plate and sat down at the table with Paul, Linda, the band, and a couple of technicians, who started listing the things they needed, such as strings and a pedal for Paul.

"So, the road manager Gerry Stickells, who was [Jimi] Hendrix's manager and stage manager for Woodstock—he was a big, burly British bloke with a rough voice—said, 'Here, son.' He gives me a couple hundred dollars. I go around the corner to the store and bring back what they need. Then he said, 'Now we need this and this.' I do it two or three times. He says to me, 'How would you like to make $125 a day?' This was 1988. I said, 'Sure.' And boom, I'm working for them the next week and a half!"

Freddy worked with the band for a couple of weeks and made friends with everyone, even doing mail runs between Eastman and Eastman, Linda's father and uncle. "I'm bringing stuff back and forth. I get to know Linda's Aunt Mary. I met the kids. At first, Paul McCartney called me Sam Ash for a couple of days. He didn't get 'Freddy' at first. Then he called me Freddy, Ready Freddy. I introduced Paul to my boss, and Paul said, 'Freddy's doing a great job for us. I might nick him from you.' And eventually he did!"

For Freddy, the excitement of that story hasn't waned in 30 years, and it doesn't end there.

Freddy carried a box of vinyl *Flowers in the Dirt* albums into a big

Broadway theater where Paul and the band were about to host a press conference. At this point, the theater was empty. Freddy walked in, and Paul called out to him from the stage. "Hey, Sam Ash, how does it sound from back there?" Only people who were working on the show were in the theater. From the back of the room, Freddy shouted back "Paul, sounds great!" "He likes to mess with you if he knows you're a fan. He'll break your chops and get a laugh out of the guys," Freddy said. "Paul says 'Do you like this one?' and he points to me, and he sings 'One, Two, Three, Four, Can't Buy Me Love.'" It still blows Freddy's mind as he tells the story.

Freddy remembers little funny times with the band and crew too. "You weren't allowed to eat meat on the premises," he said. "You had to go off premises to eat meat, and you had to buy it yourself. You couldn't bring receipts or anything, and you couldn't bring it backstage. So, once in a while the road manager would hand me a $20 bill and say 'Get two roast beef sandwiches.' Then we'd go in the broom closet and eat roast beef sandwiches! True story."

During that time Freddy met a lot of big stars, some of them before they hit the big time. "At the end of one of those rehearsals, there was a press conference," he said. "We were told to fill the theater with people. There was a quick announcement on the radio. We printed tickets from a Xerox machine! We filled the theater, and he did a one-hour concert!" During the concert, Freddy started talking to a kid with long stringy blond hair backstage. Conversations always led back to "what's your favorite Beatles song?" Freddy said, because "that's what you think of when you're watching him."

This kid said, "'Live and Let Die.'" Freddy told him that wasn't really a Beatles song and introduced himself. "The kid said, 'My name is Axl, Axl Rose [of Guns N' Roses].' They just released the record. They were nobody yet. Three months later, I saw them on TV, and I said, 'That's that guy!'"

They were a magical few years. One of Freddy's favorite takeaways from that time is the lifelong friendship he made with Wix, who is now Paul's musical director. "Whenever they're in New York, he calls me and gives me tickets. He says, 'I got two tickets; I got four tickets; I got six tickets.' I just went to the show at Grand Central. If you look through the videos, you can see the profile of my face up near the stage."

Freddy has seen Paul in concert more than 100 times between working for him and going to shows. "They're always different and always fun!"

So, how does this legacy translate to Freddy becoming Paul in a popular tribute band? It's simple. Freddy was inspired by the man himself. "I've always been a Beatles fan since I was a little kid," Freddy said. As a matter of fact, when he was about six he and his friends would play air guitar to Beatles music and "make like we're The Beatles. Little babies and our friends would watch."

"My brother was about 11 or 12. He bought the White Album. I remember being in my brother's room, and my brother was almost in tears because Paul was dead. We were looking for clues on *Sgt. Pepper* and *Abbey Road*. There was a rumor that you could call a certain telephone number and they would tell you what happened to Paul. We were looking for that phone number."

When Freddy was old enough to buy his own records, the first one he bought was *Let It Be* at a Walmart in Ridgewood, Queens, across the street from his father's restaurant. When Freddy started playing in garage bands with his friends, they were into Led Zeppelin, Aerosmith, and The Who, and that's what they wanted to play. Freddy played bass to that kind of music, but he always listened to The Beatles. "After I met Paul, I was so inspired. I developed a voice where I could sing like him and started playing in Beatles bands," Freddy said. "At first I was just singing; then I learned the bass line."

Freddy's been with the Liverpool Shuffle for close to a decade. "What's great about this band is that we all get along and have a great time. If one of us makes a mistake onstage, we can't look at each other because we'll burst out laughing."

There is no end in sight for the band. They're getting bigger and selling out popular venues that usually don't book tribute bands. "Above all, we're a family. We really respect each other's excellent musicianship. Each member has made a commitment to the music."

How long will they play? "Until people stop listening."

Sadly, the wonderful, warm Fred Giovanelli passed away before this book became a reality. Rest in peace, Freddy. You brought joy to many people.

1964 the Tribute

Mark Benson founded 1964 in 1984.

What kind of band formed in 1984 would call themselves 1964? A Beatles tribute band, of course.

Eight. Sgt. Pepper Taught the Band to Play

Based in Akron, Ohio, 1964, whose full name is 1964 The Tribute, has played Carnegie Hall 14 times, International Beatleweek in Liverpool, and the pièce de résistance, Shea Stadium. What started as something casual between musician friends has rocketed these sound-alikes to an astonishing career, becoming as close to the Beatles as many of their fans will get.

Even their genesis story is not what you would expect. They didn't start in the small club circuit. Instead, they were huge in the college market nearly right off the bat. They auditioned for the National Association of College Activities, an organization that is known for opening doors for original artists and became the first nonoriginal group to crack the code and get booked at colleges across the country. They played the college circuit for nine years, and the students couldn't get enough. The kids wanted to know more about The Beatles. They engaged band members after the shows asking if they ever saw The Beatles live or told them they wished they were born in the '60s. They wanted to know what books to buy and what movies to watch, all before the days of YouTube.

The band's popularity grew and with it the size and the importance of the venues they played. They were invited to the Deauville Hotel in Miami Beach, Florida, where the Beatles played their second performance on *The Ed Sullivan Show*. In what year? Say it with me, 1964. They played on the 50th anniversary of that day. And what could be more iconic than Shea Stadium where the Beatles played to 56,000 screaming fans on August 15, 1965? The Beatles were the first rock-and-roll group to ever play a sports stadium, and at the time it was the biggest-grossing event in show business history.

The appearance of 1964 The Tribute at Shea Stadium was a little different, but the audience still cheered. The band didn't play on the field; they played in the VIP section of the stands and were broadcast live on the Jumbo Tron. But just being in the airspace of the iconic Beatles show, playing their music, made it one of the band's most precious performances.

Mark Benson, creator of 1964 and John impersonator, was an impressionable 11-year-old when The Beatles hit the States.

"You see them on *The Ed Sullivan Show*, which is arguably the largest, most popular entertainment show on the planet at the time, and here's four guys that didn't go to college," Mark said. "They're on the biggest show in the world, and the audience is full of young girls screaming at them, and it's like wow, that's a good job."

Young people seeing guys their own age on national television opened the door to the possibility of music as a career for a lot of people. Their good looks and quick wit captivated girls and guys alike.

"As Americans, when you hear them talk, you were always charmed by their accents and their cheeky humor, which was cocky but not offensive," Mark said.

Mark echoes the sentiments of most fans when he says that The Beatles were always up for a joke. They didn't take themselves too seriously, and they gave the kind of vibe that they were fun.

Above all, what's most impressive about The Beatles is the music.

"What a lot of people missed initially is that the majority of their songs were about love or something positive," Mark said. "You could find something in almost every one of their songs that you could relate to, and that's what really grabbed me."

Mark plays John because he's always been a wise guy and thought getting paid for that would be great, he joked. What really happened was the vocal blend of original bass player and the band's cofounder Gary Grimes was very good in those two positions. Gary had an extended range that Mark didn't have; when they harmonized the sound was stunning.

"We never thought it would be full-time when we started," Mark said. "We just loved playing our favorite music. We've been going for 36 years, and there's no end in sight."

Playing Beatles music is the ultimate joy for Mark Benson. "You say to yourself 'who gets to play Carnegie Hall 14 times?' It's amazing; I do. I have a desire for people from every walk of life to see and hear this music."

Their show is based around what you would have seen if you were lucky enough to get a ticket when The Beatles were on tour, so they stay with the early material and all the songs they played live in concert.

"It's great to see the joy the music brings and to see the young people get up out of their seats and dance," Mark said.

In the new millennium, Beatles music spans the generations. Grandparents bring their grandchildren to shows. A grandfather introduced his seven-year-old grandson to The Beatles by playing Rock Band, a Beatles music video game. His grandson was hooked on the music and happily sang along in the front row of a 1964 The Tribute performance.

"Beatles music unites everyone," Mark said. "You can see three generations of a family sitting at a show. Everybody's singing, laughing, and having fun. Everyone leaves happy. There are very few types of entertainment that have that broad an appeal. There's no age group or race or economic level or political beliefs, when they come to a show, they and we are all just Beatles fans."

NINE

Obsessions Became Careers

It starts as an obsession and turns into a profession. Some fans devote their entire career to the Fab Four.

Baby, You Can Take Her Tour

Susan Ryan, tour guide of the Fab 4 NYC Walking Tours and a popular Beatles expert, said that The Beatles are a way of life. But for the woman who began her obsession at 13 in the 1970s, it took a lifetime to lead her back to where she belongs.

"I heard their music before, but when I saw them moving around, that was it!" she said, remembering the first time she saw *A Hard Day's Night* at her local library the summer before she turned 14. "When John Lennon came on the screen, it was like a duck imprinting."

That may have been when the obsession took over, but The Beatles struck a chord when Susan was little more than a toddler. She heard "We Can Work It Out" when she was just four years old. "The hook really got to me," she said. "'Life is very short and there's no time.' I was only four years old."

In those formative years, Susan remembers watching *The Beatles* cartoon on TV and seeing *Yellow Submarine* in the theater. "I don't remember a time when there wasn't Beatles music," she said. "I was little when their albums were coming out."

From that early age until the summer before Susan turned 14, The Beatles existed merely as background music for her. It was that summer at camp that changed her life. An older girl asked her if she liked The Beatles. Susan was noncommittal but said yes anyway. That older girl was a hardcore fan and wouldn't let up until Susan shared her passion. She told Susan she *had* to listen. She lent Susan her records, showed her pictures, and loaned her books. Then the public library showed *A Hard Day's Night*.

"It was all over at that point," Susan remembers with a smile. "It was visceral. It's a gut thing. You want more. You need more. You die if you don't get more."

Susan was completely obsessed in the '70s when it was so uncool. "I got such grief for it," she recalls. "I feel vindicated now."

Susan cracked the old boy network and is now a well-known Beatles expert. She knew she had finally arrived when Mark Lewisohn, considered the most learned author on The Beatles, told her she knew her stuff.

Susan is an organizer and speaker at the Fest for Beatle Fans, previously known as Beatlefest, now in its 50th year, a twice-annual three-day fest that honors the lasting legacy of The Beatles. The festival takes place in the New York metropolitan area, ordinarily in March or April, and in Chicago, Illinois, each August. The Fest didn't happen in 2020 because of the worldwide pandemic.

Susan's teenage years were tough. Teens in the '70s thought the band was old hat, broken up, and, worse yet, boring. She got teased for loving John; her classmates would say "He's old enough to be your father."

Susan found her tribe when, at 15, she went to her first Fest. It was in Manhattan, just a short train ride from where she lived in Queens, but she was not allowed to ride the train by herself. Her protective dad called the Fest's founder, Mark Lapidos, to see if it was safe for his baby. Mark reassured him, and despite his trepidations, her dad let her go. "My dad was not a current pop culture guy," she said. "He was into pop culture from his time. But he got The Beatles thing. It was uncharacteristic of him to say I could go."

Still, the train was too dangerous. Her dad drove Susan and her friend. They were allowed to go for only the first night, and they couldn't stay late. Susan could feel the minutes ticking by. "It was like a game," she recalls. "We brought 50 bucks with us. And the game was to see how much stuff you could get and still bring money back."

It was at this Fest that Susan and her friend first realized they weren't alone in their passion for The Beatles. Susan had found her people. "It got to be if there was any Beatles event within 10 miles of New York City, I would know 10 people," she said. "You develop circles. The world of Beatles people was small at that time."

As Susan got older she took full advantage of living close to John and Yoko, who were in Manhattan. Now old enough to ride the big bad train, she went to the Dakota building on every school break and waited for a glimpse of John. She never did get that glimpse.

Eventually her love for the band led Susan to her husband, Jim. He reminded her of the love of her life, John.

The early part of her relationship with her future husband was on-again, off-again. Every time she dated someone else, she would compare him to Jim. Susan was looking for someone smart like John Lennon. Soon she realized that Jim was the only man who measured up. The couple have been married almost 30 years.

December 8, 1980, the night John Lennon was murdered by Mark David Chapman, is etched in indelible ink in Susan's mind. "I was in my dorm at Hofstra [a small private college on Long Island, New York] watching reruns of *M*A*S*H*. At 11:00 that night, my roommate's boyfriend came in and gave us the news. He said John had been shot outside the Dakota. I sat up in bed and screamed. A friend called from another dorm and said come over. I listened all night to the radio. He [the friend] was crying, and I was crying. There was a gathering on campus. We all signed a scroll to give to Yoko."

Cut to 30 years later, the long and winding road that led Susan to becoming the NYC walking tour guide.

Before Susan and Jim's now-adult son, James, was born, Susan worked as an executive assistant at publishing houses and public relations companies. She stopped working outside the home to be a stay-at-home mom. At the same time, Susan's friend was running the walking tours. She asked Susan to be her backup and run the tours when she couldn't. Eventually her friend moved to Los Angeles, and Susan made the tours her own, bringing her own unique stories to each Beatles location. The tour includes the Ed Sullivan Theater, Strawberry Fields, the Dakota building and lesser-known Beatles locations, all colored with stories only Susan can tell.

In 2007, Susan appeared on a DVD called *John Lennon's New York*. She is also mentioned in Candy Leonard's book *Beatleness*, Al Sussman's book *Changin' Times: 101 Days That Shaped a Generation*, and May Pang's *Instamatic Karma*. Recently Susan coauthored a book titled *The Beatles Fab Four Cities: Liverpool, Hamburg, London, New York*.

Forty years after that summer at camp, Susan has made a career out of being a number one Beatles fan.

They're Getting Better All the Time

You would think that the executive editor of *Beatlefan* magazine, a man who wrote the book *Changin' Times: 101 Days That Shaped a Generation* and was cohost of the *Things We Said Today* Beatles radio show, had always been a Beatles fan. As a matter of fact, he was not. The first time Al Sussman heard the number one hit "I Want to Hold Your Hand," he didn't like it. It was something he had never heard before, and his reaction was far from positive. The day after he heard it all the girls at school were talking about The Beatles, and he just didn't get it, he said.

Eventually, seeing the mop tops on television won him over. "It was their show from Miami Beach where they were onstage in a hotel ballroom," he recalled. "They were very close to each other. It was only a few months before that that they were playing [small] ballrooms [in England]. They were in their element. It was the way the sound was set up. Ringo's drums and Paul's bass were dominant. They wore down my resistance."

The day after that television appearance, Al bought the three singles that were available. He was 14. "I may as well have had a target on my back," he joked. He was their audience.

When Al hit high school, The Beatles were huge. In 1965, there was no shadow of a doubt who the biggest pop act was. On April 4, 1964, The Beatles had the top five positions on the *Billboard* top 100: "Can't Buy Me Love," "Twist and Shout," "She Loves You," "I Want to Hold Your Hand," and "Please Please Me." "You just have to look at the footage of what it was like in a two-block radius of any hotel they stayed at in Manhattan. The entire two blocks on any side of the hotel were paralyzed," he said.

At 14, Al had no inkling that his love for the band would shape his career and his entire life.

Fresh out of high school, with his finger on the pulse of the teen scene, Al started a column called "Teen Center" in the local paper in Maywood, New Jersey. He would write about what was going on around town and, of course, what was going on musically. Music always involved The Beatles. After all, it was the late '60s and early '70s. Al catapulted from the small-town paper to becoming a freelance writer for one of the first Beatles fanzines, *The Right Thing*.

Then came the move that changed Al's life. It seemed small at the time; no one can predict what the future holds. In 1979, Al picked up a *Beatlefan* magazine while attending a Beatlefest. In it was a notice that publisher Bill Kane was looking for a New York correspondent. Al knew this was the place for him. Kane agreed. Al's first piece appeared in the last issue of the magazine's first year. This was his true calling. He has been with the magazine for nearly 40 years and now bears the title of executive editor.

Beatlemania Lives On

As with all true Beatles fans, the band's effect didn't stop with Al's career. The Beatles seeped into his personal life. In the early '70s, Al took a job at the now-defunct Sam Goody record store in Paramus, New Jersey. It was there that he met lifelong friend and Fest for Beatles Fans founder Mark Lapidos. As a department clerk on his first day, Al met the record department manager, Mark. "The first two things he said to me were 'Never run out of Beatles records' and 'Listen to WABC-FM radio tonight to hear a new singer-songwriter—Elton John.'"

"I was one of the first people Mark told about his idea for the now more than 40-year–running Beatlefest," said Al. "The first one was held September 8 and 9, 1974, at what was then the Commodore Hotel, now the Grand Hyatt." More than 40 years later Al still helps Mark run the event, which attracts about 6,000 fans annually from around the world.

Al has been lucky enough to see Paul with Wings and solo and Ringo Starr and His All-Starr Band in concert several times. While those were mind-blowing experiences, Al still kicks himself about a lost opportunity to see the four together in concert back in the day:

Word had gotten around with the male Beatles fans that the concerts were not too satisfying. You couldn't hear anything but girls screaming. I remember the morning of the second time they played Shea Stadium in 1966. It wasn't sold out. There was an ad in the *Daily News* for the show. I thought, being in Jersey, it was a schlep to Shea. I wouldn't be able to hear, and they'd be back next year. Six days later, they did their last concert at Candlestick Park.

The saving grace of the story is that Al met Ringo at a book signing at Tower Records (another memory in the record world) near Lincoln Center. "I said, 'Great to meet you,' and we shook hands. It was great!"

You can't pin Al down on a favorite Beatle or a favorite song. "My favorite Beatles song is whatever I just heard," he quipped. "The same with my favorite Beatle—it's whoever we're talking about or listening to."

The Beatles are four parts of a whole. And 50 years after the band broke up, the music and the memories live through fans such as Al Sussman.

TEN

Ladies and Gentlemen,
The Beatles

Thousands of fans were lucky enough to see the boys live onstage. Listen to these women tell their stories of watching their true loves in real life.

Something in the Way They Moved

She saw The Beatles live at Shea Stadium.

"When it was all over, everyone was crying. Some girls peed their pants!" But Bobbie Molina of the Bronx, then 13, didn't shed a tear when she saw The Beatles at Shea Stadium in 1965. She felt feet on her shoulders as people stepped over her to try to get closer to the lads as they left the stadium, but she never took her eyes off the boys. She was mesmerized. Crying was a waste of time. She knew how fleeting and how important it was to see the boys play live in person. She soaked in every head shake, every hand gesture, every drumbeat. The sound system was

Julian Lennon and Bobbie Molina, April 14, 2019.

awful. She could only vaguely hear the music. But that wasn't important. They were actually in front of her. She could see them moving
around not too far in the distance. Now, at 69, she recalls every detail as
if it were yesterday.

Bobbie's passion for The Beatles saved her from a lifetime of home-
sickness. Her family moved to the Bronx just one year before The Beatles exploded onto the scene on *The Ed Sullivan Show* on February 9,
1964. She was born in rural Texas, where her father was stationed in
the military. He retired when she was 12, and Bobbie and her family
were uprooted from their hometown and dropped into his hometown
of the Boogie Down Bronx. Nothing would ever be the same. She was
homesick for wide-open spaces and her friends back in the Lone Star
State. Sure, she started meeting friends slowly when she went to school,
but the Bronx was not home in her heart. Her family settled into a routine. Like millions of families across the country, after Sunday dinner
they would sit down in front of the television and watch *The Ed Sullivan Show*.

"All of a sudden, these guys are singing," Bobbie told me, almost as
excited as she was nearly 60 years ago. "Who are they?" The words fell
from her lips as she watched the lads on the screen:

> I was captured like a magnet to the TV—the music and the songs. Then they
> did close-ups. I couldn't believe how cute they were. Their expressions were
> too much. I looked at the drummer. He was so cute and funny. I liked all of
> them. Paul was great-looking. John was great-looking too, but it said "Sorry,
> girls, he's married" on the bottom of the screen. So he was out of the way.
> We had no chance with him.

Ringo captured Bobbie's fancy. "His goofy smile, the way he swayed
his head back and forth, his hair. His big nose. It was a turn-on. It was a
different face that I never saw before. His character, his body language
really drew me in. He was sexy even though I was only 13. Even though
he wasn't singing, it was his movements that got me."

Bobbie went to school the next day and discovered her new best
friend was in love with the boys too. Bobbie's passion took over; she had
no more room in her heart to be homesick.

Bobbie started collecting Beatles bubblegum cards with secret info
on the backs of their pictures—important facts such as their favorite
colors, their favorite movies, and, most importantly, what they liked in
girls. Bobbie started hanging around the candy store to be the first in
line for the newest cards. The four lads from Liverpool graced the covers of all the fan magazines. Bobbie was hooked on *16 Magazine,* which

always had thrilling articles filled with the latest gossip about her heart-throbs. Every month she would run to the store to be sure she got there before they sold out.

It wasn't long before the magazines had pictures of the boys' girlfriends. "Paul had Jane Asher, and Ringo had Maureen. I was jealous, but I wanted to know all about them. They had bangs and straight hair. I thought maybe they [The Beatles] would like me if I looked them." Bobbie straightened her hair, bought a black turtleneck, and even tried for an English accent. Her teenage dream was to take a trip to London after graduation and meet her boys. It didn't come true.

But another dream did. Bobbie saw girls winning prizes in a contest called Dreamsville in *16 Magazine*. Prizes included T-shirts and lockets, but she was going big. She picked up a pen and paper and wrote "Dear Dreamsville Contest, I'm requesting four tickets to see The Beatles when they come to New York." She asked for four because, being a young teen, she thought her parents would take her and her sister. "It was very simple. I mailed it. I didn't think I would get a response. I thought it was too much to ask."

A month later, there was a letter in the mailbox addressed to her. The return address? *16 Magazine.* "It couldn't be!" she squealed, reliving the moment. "I opened it, and four yellow tickets fell out. The letter said, 'Dear Barbara (that's my real name)—Congratulations! You just won four tickets to see The Beatles in concert in New York City, August 15, 1965, at Shea Stadium.'"

Bobbie ran up two flights of stairs to the apartment she now called home. She spread the news to her family. Her older sister, Nanna, wasn't a big Beatles fan, but the music played on the radio as she applied her makeup and sprayed her hair getting ready for school every morning. "How you gonna go?" she said, bursting Bobbie's bubble.

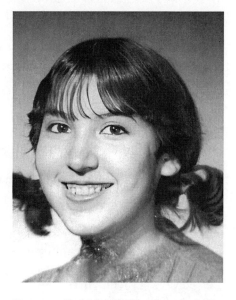

Teenage Bobbie Molina around the time she saw The Beatles at Shea Stadium, 1965.

193

Bobbie's father was a tough sell. She had to pull out all the stops, begging and pleading and putting on her best pout. Her father finally caved when her cousin, who was all of 17, said she would take 13-year-old Bobbie. She was going!

Bobbie anxiously counted down the long months until August. One day, miraculously, she turned the calendar and it read August 15. The four boarded the subway for the short trip from the Bronx into Queens, where Shea Stadium was located.

The subway was buzzing with excitement. "There were lots of girls giggling and laughing, and they had banners," Bobbie recalled. "When we got closer to Shea, we saw so many cars. There were so many girls wearing Beatles buttons. We heard the screams 'We want The Beatles!'"

Bobbie and her entourage made it into the huge stadium. She had no idea where they were sitting or what exactly was going on. With her rural roots, she had never been to a baseball stadium before. She couldn't believe her luck. They were seated right down front. An usher had to shoo away some kids who were trying to steal their seats. Everyone above them had banners saying "We Love the Beatles," "We Love Ringo," and "We Love Paul."

"It was Beatles heaven. It was all Beatles fans. We were all in the same boat. Everyone together. It was like a huge family wanting them," Bobbie said.

Much to the crowd's dismay, there were several opening acts. Famed New York DJ Murray the K introduced them all. He said "Murray the K and the swinging soiree," just like he said on the radio. Martha and the Vandellas sang "Dancing in the Streets," the Rascals sang a couple of songs, and all the while the crowd was screaming "We want The Beatles!"

Finally, Ed Sullivan came onstage. A hush fell over the crowd as The Beatles came running out of the dugout. For Bobbie, the scene was in slow motion.

"You could see the mopheads. Then there was a scream from the belly of the crowd," Bobbie said:

There was one head in particular that looked like it was light auburn, almost reddish. It must have been John Lennon. Their hair was so beautiful. It was so shiny and gleaming under the lights of Shea Stadium. They ran up to the stage, one, two, three. They got to their instruments and started tuning them. Then, really quick, they said, "Hello, hello, hello." They started jamming. I think their first song was "Twist and Shout." Everyone started screaming and crying. Everyone was so happy!

Bobbie was so close that she fantasized the boys could see her.

When Paul turned in her direction toward left field, she waved and waved. Then he waved. She was sure he was waving to her. "There's a picture that was captured of him waving to left field, and I'm saying that's when he was waving to me."

What we have seen in the films and on YouTube Bobbie saw in real life. Fans jumped over the fence. One girl almost made it to the stage. Ringo turned around. Then the cops got her. John even said she almost made it.

"It was just terrific. I couldn't believe it was actually them there," Bobbie said. She continued: "When the concert was over, a station wagon pulled up, and they went in. It's a slow-motion memory. Instead of screaming, I focused on them. They were headed to the picnic area, toward my way. As the car passed, they got closer to me. I'm not sure which Beatle it was, but he took out a white handkerchief and waved it up and down saying goodbye. They were maybe 20 feet away. The rest of The Beatles were waving goodbye too. All of a sudden, they left the stadium. When they left, everyone collapsed, crying and hysterical. I didn't cry. I didn't even scream. I kept everything to myself. I didn't talk to my sister or my cousin. I captured every movement, everything I saw. I didn't take my face off of them at all. As people climbed over my shoulders to get closer, the cops stopped every one of them. I think about it now, and I know I could've really gotten hurt."

To this day, Bobbie is dying to know which Beatle was waving that handkerchief.

That wasn't Bobbie's last brush with the boys. Almost 50 years later, she came face to face with the love of her life, Ringo Starr, at a gallery exhibiting his artwork. When he entered the room the crowd parted, and Bobbie placed herself in the front. "I said, 'Hello, Ringo,' and I touched his shoulder. It took me so many years to see him again in person. Here I am, an old, grown woman."

When Ringo left the crowd parted again, and Bobbie was sure not to let anyone push her out of her front-row position. "I said, 'Goodbye, Ringo,' and touched him on the other side of his shoulder."

The magic won't stop there if Bobbie has anything to do with it. The woman who started the Facebook group The Beatles, The Best Band Ever, which boasts over 5,000 members, plans on taking her pen in hand again and writing an old-fashioned letter to Paul McCartney in London.

"It would be the greatest prize in the world to receive a letter from Paul McCartney," she sighed. "I would die happy."

Cry Baby Cry

> She cried her eyes out when she saw
> The Beatles live in Chicago.

A screamer or a crier? Did you ever ask yourself what you would be if you were a teenage girl at a Beatles concert? Karen Stoessel, 70, of Schaumburg, Illinois, was a crier.

"I cried because I couldn't reach them. I couldn't touch them," Karen said. "I was so sure that if he [Paul] met me, that would've been it. Sometimes I still tell people if Paul would have only met me before he met Linda, or Heather, or Nancy."

Back when Karen was 13 and saw them for the first time, she "was convinced, just convinced, that no other girl in that stadium that was screaming for Paul or held a sign for Paul loved him as much as me. So I had that going for me." The concert was more than 50 years ago, but she remembers it as if it were yesterday. She got to see The Beatles twice! She was 13 the first time and about 16 the second time. "I was much more mature the second time," she laughs. "I knew much, much, much more about being in love."

That first time Karen was just a kid. "I bought a program; I remember that. I don't remember how much it cost, and the poor man that was sitting one row below us really got a banging on his head," Karen remembered. "I was so excited. I had rolled it [the program] up, and I was hitting the poor man on top of his head! After a while he was like, 'Look,' but I think he realized what and where he was. So, they were out there, and I just sat there and cried. I was so excited."

Karen's girlfriend Ruth was a George girl, but "I was a Paul girl," Karen said, adding that the concert seemed fast, almost as if they were there and then they were gone: "I didn't hear them. I heard just screaming. And then the one thing I do remember—I'll never, ever, ever, forget—was when they were finished and Paul took off his Höfner, and he grabbed it by the chords or whatever it's called [neck]. He picked it up and waved it and was looking toward the first base line, and I knew he was waving to me! Not anyone—not the other 6,000 girls in that section—he was waving to me, and I just cried."

She felt weak, Karen recalled, and before she knew it, The Beatles were gone. "They were off the stage. And now I had to walk. We had to leave. I was in another state. Even thinking about it now chokes me up. I was in such heaven, and my poor girlfriend Ruth, I remember she had a jacket on with a hood, and she looked at me and she said, 'Karen ...'

There were masses of people. She said, 'Karen, hold on to my hood, and don't let go.' I was just in another state. She just led me by her hood out of that park. I couldn't talk. I was crying. I was just—I was out of it. We walked back to the L [train], and we went home, and I was never really the same after that."

For lots of people, seeing The Beatles live is the experience of a lifetime. But not for Karen. The boys came back to Chicago a couple of years later, and that time she somehow got really good seats for herself and three girlfriends:

"We weren't on the main floor. We were one level up from the stage, and our seats were on the side where Paul played. I could see him really well, and luckily our seats were dead center under a speaker. In those days, it was like a tin can. Oh my God, they [the speakers] were awful, but we could hear them above all the screaming. We could actually hear them because it was right over our head. And I was much more ... I was crying. I was upset. But I didn't bean anybody that was in front of me. Of course, I had another program, but by this time I couldn't even think of rolling it because the condition of my program from the first concert—I think it's still curved. So, I made sure it stayed really nice and flat."

This time, Karen took her brother's advice and brought binoculars:

"My brother had these incredible binoculars that he brought back from Germany. He was stationed over the during the '60s. And so he trusted me with his binoculars, and I had them hanging around my neck. So, there were four girls. There was my girlfriend Pat, who is my oldest friend I have. She was a Ringo girl. There was Maryellen, who was a George girl, and then there was Judy. Judy was a Paul girl ... another Paul girl! And we all know that Paul loves me more. I remember this too. I had those binoculars. I was looking at them. And they were so good. I mean, you could see the blackheads on Paul's nose. They were really good, and we had those good seats. So, my girlfriend Pat, who was the Ringo girl, I let her look at them. And then my girlfriend Maryellen, who liked George, I let her. And then my girlfriend Judy, who was like 'Lemme look! Lemme look at Paul!' I wouldn't let her look at them because I knew she was gonna be looking at Paul. We're still [the] best of friends now, and we laugh about it all the time. I just wouldn't because I knew she was gonna look at him, and I didn't want her to.

So, that was the concert. Judy got me back because she and Pat left early. They got up out of their seats, and they got to The Beatles' car at some point. I don't know how. I didn't even know they were gone because I couldn't take my eyes off of Paul. But then they [the Beatles] left the stage, and all of a sudden I was like where did they [Karen's friends] go? And we met up and talked later. They had gotten close to the car and saw them leave the stadium! So she got me. She had a better view of Paul than I did."

All four girls grew up and stayed best friends. When they were in their 20s, Karen and Judy were roommates. Judy loved to hear Karen make up fan fiction stories about Paul. The stories were always about different situations where each of the four friends met their favorite Beatle.

Karen said her love for Paul has been in her DNA since the early days. She got to meet a Beatles insider when she was working as a secretary in the music department at her local community college. Barry Miles was one of The Beatles' chauffeurs. He spoke to an English class at the community college, and the teacher invited Karen since she was a well-known Beatles junkie. Karen brought her friend and Beatles author Kit O'Toole. Karen said,

> I'm so awestruck when I see someone like that. The first thing I said to that man when I met him, "Would you tell Paul about me?" Barry was very close to them, and, of course, he wrote a book. He laughed. I said to Kit, "Of course that's the only thing I could say to that man."
>
> That's my life with Paul. I still love him. I still cry when I see him on TV and when I hear his music. I have seen him at almost every tour he goes on. I've been in third row seats where I got hit on the head by a guitar pick!

At the same concert, there was a crane with a basket on it. Paul and Linda were in the basket and hovered above the first five or six rows. "I was almost able to touch his shoe! I was soooooo ... but I didn't. And that's what breaks my heart. Because I can get so far, but then I just can't. I could never reach him."

Karen has tried desperately to get closer to Paul by taking six trips to London to look for him. On one of those trips, she got painfully close. "I never sought out actively going to his house until we actually went to his house in St. John's Wood. I was like *This is it. I'm ringing the door-bell, I'm going in. I'm meeting him.*" Paul's house was like a fortress in the middle of the city. Karen saw milk bottles by the front door. Her first thought was to nick one of the bottles. She thought that would be the biggest prize. Her conscience took over, and she realized she would be taking milk from Paul's young children. Instead she took one of the empties.

Karen said, "The house in St. John's Wood was very accessible. There was a wall, and the doors into his property were green. You could very clearly see the house. The house from the brick wall to the street was about 50 or 60 feet. It wasn't that far. It was so wildly, colorfully painted, it looked like a circus. Pink windows, really crazy. You knew it was Paul's house. There was no security. My girlfriend and I were the only two people there. I don't think he stayed there a lot in St. John's Wood. He probably had another place that maybe had more security. But that was it. That was his house. You can see pictures of him in it.

The best part of that trip—not only did I get that milk bottle, and I got it home safely. *I held his cat!* His cat came over the wall. I saw a picture of it in a book. I held that cat, and my girlfriend took a picture of me with his cat!"

It was Paul's eyes that drew Karen to him that night in February 1964:

"Those eyes, and that smile, and when he shook that head, that just took my heart away. He grabbed it that moment, and he's had it ever since. I still smile a lot when I see him on TV or a picture in a magazine or online somewhere. He makes me feel warm and fuzzy, almost like he's family because he's been with me so long—since I was 13, and I'm gonna be 70. He's been with me every day in some way."

The Crowd Rushed the Stage—The Beatles Stopped the Show

Bonnie Granato
(In Her Own Words)

Cleveland, 1966. My ticket cost $5.50, which was a lot of money for a girl who got $1.00 a week allowance. I asked my mother for a loan and went five and a half weeks without so much as a 10-cent chocolate Coke. It was worth it! It rained the whole two-hour trip to Cleveland and most of that day prior to show time. Once we reached Cleveland, we had to go through the downtown area to get to the stadium. There were race riots happening, and the streets were full of people. It was quite scary, as our car was surrounded. We made it through without incident and finally arrived. A cousin of the girl we went with had stood in line all night and got us front-row tickets. We felt disappointment when we saw how huge the stadium was and how far we actually were from that stage. I remember the Cyrkle & Bobby Heb singing "Sunny" but don't remember any of the other groups, as we were there to see a phenomenon that we had never witnessed before. About 15 minutes after The Beatles came on, the security fence was broken down, and the crowd rushed the stage. You could barely breathe due to the pushing and shoving. It was mass hysteria, to say the least. My leg was caught between other fans' legs, and kids were actually climbing and standing on our legs for a better view. Some of the guys were grabbing girls' breasts because there was nothing you could do to get away from it. The Beatles were taken offstage and would NOT be brought back out unless everyone returned to their seats. Once the massive, frenzied crowd returned to their seats, the fence was erected again. Looking back down on the field was a sea of trampled clothing, crushed umbrellas, broken cameras, shoes, etc. The Beatles

Bonnie Granato, 2019 photograph with her ticket from a Beatles concert in the '60s.

returned and began playing. Who knows what song it was because you could never hear them. The fence was broken down again, and I made it to the front of the stage. The Beatles are laughing, and Paul motions the girls forward. I jumped up and touched his boot and got hit with a policeman's billy club. I did see stars! They took them offstage, and the concert was over. The next day at school I was covered with bruises from the frenzied crowd and had a big goose egg on my forehead that I was very proud of. It was the night of my life!!

Eleven

This and That

You've heard their stories. Many Beatles fans born after the 1960s feel like they don't fit in. The following two stories did not fit into any category I planned, but they are so good that I could not leave them out.

That Boy

I've just seen a face—or have I? It's the face that makes fans swoon, follow him through trains, and stutter as they ask for selfies. Sometimes fans walk away, thinking they have met the famous Beatle. But alas, it's not Paul—it's John. Not that John. He asked me not to use his last name for business reasons.

John M.'s sister noticed it as soon as The Beatles hit *The Ed Sullivan Show*. "You look like Paul," she told him. He couldn't help but see the resemblance. The fandom didn't start until many years later, after the band broke up. John M. went to his sister's hairdresser, and she insisted he change his hair to the shaggy look that Paul was sporting. After that, it didn't stop.

People never chased John M. down the street or ripped his clothing. It's more subtle than that, especially these days. It's the little things. "When I walk down the street [in Manhattan], everyone says hello," John M. said. "I think maybe they're acknowledging this Paul McCartney lookalike, or maybe they're acknowledging a face, and they don't quite know where it goes to."

A scene taken right out of *A Hard Day's Night* once occurred. John M. recalled:

I was on 14th Street changing for a train to go further downtown. There was a group of young people—late 20s, early 30s—in the middle of the platform, and they were French. As I'm watching for the train to come, I see them all looking in my direction. I didn't think anything about it, but then my second sense said *Y'know, there's something a little strange here.* When the train came, they all made a mad dash to get into my car. They

201

all sat at the one end, and I went to the extreme other end. After about one stop, one of the fellas came over and he said, "Can myself and my girl-friend take a photo of you?"

I said, "For what?"

He said, "It's okay if you don't want to say who you are, but can we take a photo with you?"

And I said, "All right."

So they came on over and they took a selfie, and before I know it they went back, and then the whole rest of them came on over, and then I found two girls on one side and a fella on the other. They all wanted to make this connection. After a while, they all took a photo. And I said, "Okay that's enough." I said, "I have other things I have to think about."

They all said goodbye. Then when I got out they got out, and that's when it got a little crazy. I went up the stairs and they stayed a good distance behind, but as soon as I made a mad dash outside, they made a mad dash.... I caught a cab. I had to get out of there.

That was the first time being spotted as Paul bothered John. M. "It's a fact that if you're a celebrity, you really don't have any privacy."

John M. has stories of people buying him drinks in bars and eye-ing him from across the room. He always tells people he's not Paul—complete with his American accent. But who knows what people think?

The famous face has helped build John M.'s career. It makes peo-ple he meets feel comfortable right away, and, of course, it's a face they never forget. "[Strangers] look at me with a glimmer in their eyes," John M. said. "It looks as if they're saying 'You either are or you're not, but there's something here.'"

Even today, The Beatles still have a huge following in Japan. When John M. was in his late 30s, he and his wife were invited to do a college lecture circuit in five cities. The seminars were about inspiration and where ideas come from. "In three of the cities, at the end of the lecture, the girls came up to me," John M. said. "They knew I wasn't, but they said, 'You know, you look like Paul McCartney.' The funny thing is they were so in awe of what I looked like, they couldn't answer or talk about any questions. They were tongue-tied."

On a typical New York City day, John M. will be going up the stairs in the subway and someone will say hi. "I just say, 'Hi.'"

"Paul's persona has always been someone who is accessible, not angry or upset or does crazy things to people who approach him. I think all of that has been a positive experience for my own life."

With a Little Help from His Friends

He produced a live Beatles show ... well, almost. Mike Fitelson is the executive director at the United Palace of Cultural Arts in New York. The United Palace is an interfaith spiritual center, entertainment venue, and artistic hub in the heart of Washington Heights. Built in 1930 as a grand movie theater and one of five Loew's Wonder Theatres, the United Palace is famous for its eclectic architectural styles, classic motifs, and international decorative touches.

"We're all about honoring the building's past," Mike said. "We always have a live element when we show a movie. In the old days, there was always live entertainment, a newsreel, a short, maybe a cartoon, and then the feature." Back in 2014 when the theater began showing movies again after a 40-year hiatus, Lin-Manuel Miranda brought in Broadway singers. When the theater showed the movie *Ghostbusters*, actors dressed as ghostbusters were on the stage before the screening.

So, after Mike ran into the popular New York Beatles tribute band Strawberry Fields, he said he always kept them in his back pocket. Then in September of 2018, it all came together. Mike got the license to show *A Hard Day's Night*, with Strawberry Fields as the opening act. When asked why now he simply said, "The Beatles now and forever."

Mike, born in 1969, was on this earth for only one month while The Beatles were together. Still, the music is on the playlist of his life. "I and a lot of other people feel we missed the organic newness; we missed the music unfolding in real time," he said. "A tribute band preserves the live music. Seeing a tribute band feels really special."

Mike loves the music, but what he loves most about The Beatles is their story:

"The human arc and the musical development are things you can very easily glom onto any story of life. I know people who were 12, 13, 14 years old when "Please Please Me" came out, and that was it. Their life was marked. It was a signpost as to who they were as a person at that time. Then when they were in their early to late 20s, The Beatles lost sight of each other at the same time that those people lost sight and let go of what they had before."

Mike has Beatles memories from long before he became a fan:

"I had a babysitter, and somehow she found my parents' copy of *Sgt. Pepper.* So, you open up the cover and there's a picture of the four of them. She thought I had the same profile as one of them; I don't remember which. So, she shined a light on me, cast a shadow on the wall, traced a profile of my face, and said, 'See? You're whoever.'

Another time after that, my family and I used to go to a cabin in Fresno, California. I have a cousin who is a year older than me, and she holed up in the attic and listened to all The Beatles music, wall to wall, cover to cover."

"The music is one thing," Mike said. "But the story is so strong. No band has an arc as compelling as The Beatles. The weirdest thing in the world is that the Rolling Stones are still playing."

Mike's not old enough to remember, but he told the story of when, in 1977, Lorne Michaels went live on *Saturday Night Live* and offered The Beatles some ridiculous (small) amount of money (it was $3,000) to reunite:

> Paul tells the story that he was over at John's house, and he said to John, "Let's go down and collect our money."
>
> And John said, "No, I'm too tired."
>
> If that story is real, it's the perfect punctuation mark on The Beatles story. It punctures all myths and speculations about The Beatles post–*Abbey Road* that they all hated each other. It had just run its course.

Epilogue

I Don't Really Want to Stop the Show

And in the end ... there is no end. I'm writing this epilogue when I could be writing 10 more essays. The story of The Beatles is endless. Recounting the stories of their fans around the world, while extremely enjoyable, is impossible to complete.

I know this much is true: The Beatles, their music, and their message of love and peace bring joy. Their inadvertent message of being true to yourself makes anyone who feels like an outsider suddenly feel welcome and part of a community. Their message of inclusion regardless of race, gender, or sexual orientation is something the entire world community should embrace.

The Beatles' music, from its simplest to its most complex, is something that will be studied and celebrated for eternity. Their lyrics will be dissected and will influence writers and poets until time stands still.

Ultimately, the task of explaining the enormity of The Beatles, how they changed music and the world, is inconceivable. Words cannot describe what those four men together were. Like the universe itself, it was pure magic. It was The Beatles.

Index

Index